SECOND EDITION

Growing Toward Intimacy

HELPING CATHOLIC TEENS INTEGRATE SPIRITUALITY & SEXUALITY

BY BOB BARTLETT

Good Ground Press

Sisters of St. Joseph of Carondelet
1884 Randolph Avenue St. Paul, Minnesota 55105
1-800-232-5533 goodgroundpress.com

Acknowledgements

Special thanks to Anne Marie, Mike Shimek,
my dad, the late Bob Bartlett, Sr., and my mother Alyce.

Graphic Design
Linda Andreozzi, Cabin 6

Photography: Cleo Freelance Photography: 28, 68, 96; James Shaffer 13, 39, 58, 67, 86, 92; Oscar Williams: 81, 89, 112, 120; W. P. Wittman Limited: Cover: top left, center right, 43. All other photos by Editorial Development Associates.

ISBN: 1-895996-05-5
Nihil Obstat: James M. Lavin
Imprimatur: Harry J. Flynn, D.D., Archbishop of St. Paul-Minneapolis,
April 8, 2002
The Nihil Obstat and Imprimatur are official declarations that a book or pamphlet is free of doctrinal or moral error. No implication is contained therein that those who have granted the Nihil Obstat and Imprimatur agree with the content, opinions, or statements expressed.

Contents

Foreword

Shortly after graduating from college, I took a job as a parish youth minister. I loved the work and felt I was doing wonderful things for God—holding Bible discussions, doing Confirmation programs, retreats, working on music and drama in liturgies. I was young. People in the parish were introducing me to their daughters and nieces.

My honeymoon as a youth minister went on for six months until a high school sophomore visited me, seeking help with a problem regarding sexuality. I did not know then how her visit permanently changed my life. This dimension of youth ministry was as messy and scary as the rest of the work was clear-cut and exciting.

I did the best I could to help this young woman. But I made it explicitly clear to God that I didn't want any more young people coming to my door with problems in the sexuality area. I did a great imitation of Jeremiah. "I am too young. Send someone else." And a Moses imitation, "I am not qualified. My brother would do a much better job."

The clearer I made my request to God, the more young people came. People say that God works in strange, mysterious ways. This is a nice way of saying God does not consult. God does not set up an appointment, walk through the wall, and ask, "Where do you want to be in the next 10 years? Let's map this out."

God did not listen to me. Soon I found myself dealing with girls who were pregnant, guys whose girlfriends were pregnant, sexually-transmitted diseases, rape, date rape, incest, homosexuality, and areas not yet identified by the social sciences.

I also ran into the flip side of the above problems. High school students desperately wondering what they had to do to get a date came to me.

"Bob, I'm a senior (substitute junior or sophomore) and I've never been out on a date. I'm beginning to wonder if I ever will. I'm wondering where I might get a body transplant or a personality transplant."

I always nodded supportively and said, "Let's talk." Often these kids need to appreciate who they really are.

I enrolled in a master's program in counseling/psychology with a specialization in human sexuality at a local college. As teens continued to come and talk, the thought dawned on me (I am not famous for quickness) that someone should be talking with them before things got so bad. I recruited some excellent parish volunteers. Together we created and offered sexuality retreats to the parish. These retreats provided a safe forum where kids could be forthright, honest, and vulnerable about their relationships and dating. They could talk with peers and caring adults about highlights and lowlights in relationships, ask questions, vent frustrations, and discover that they were not alone.

The local public schools heard about what we were doing from some of our kids and invited me to come and speak to their health classes. I made no mention of God, of course. These early events were the beginning of a fascinating journey still taking me places I never dreamed. Today I am grateful to God, the many teens who shared their stories and struggles with me, and the others at the parish. They have taught me. Sexuality can be a source of confusion, frustration, and pain for teens. I hope this book offers some insight and wisdom. Much of the material for this book comes from conversations, counseling sessions, and classroom discussions with teens who have been willing to share their successes, struggles, insights, and pain in regard to sexuality.

Many teens believe they are alone in what they experience and believe about sex and sexuality. This book will dispel that myth.

CHAPTER 1

Sex Is Not Just a Biological need

What contradictory attitudes toward sex do you see around you? Find expressions of these attitudes in music, film, advertisements, magazines.

"The power and pleasure that are part of sexuality demand of us the intelligence, honesty, and sacrifice that test our maturity. But we do not fear sexuality; we embrace it. What we fear at times is our own inability to think as highly of the gift as does the God who made us sexual beings."

—*Bishop Francis Mugavero*

Sex is sacred. This is the teaching of the Catholic Church. In our culture that uses sex to sell cars and increase ticket sales to the movies, the Church's teaching is prophetic. It calls teens to integrate their sexuality and their spirituality, to become whole and holy adults capable of loving relationships.

In his article "Reuniting Sexuality and Spirituality," moral theologian James B. Nelson says the roots of sexual sin lie in alienation—the failure to integrate opposing tendencies within ourselves.

For example, if we fail to integrate body and spirit, the body becomes just a sensation machine to be feared or enjoyed. In the Victorian era of the late 19th century, men and women wore high collars, long sleeves, and voluminous clothes to lock the body in safety. Today, the *Playboy* philosophy holds the opposite view—the body is a pleasure machine. Both the Victorian and the *Playboy* attitudes split body and spirit.

Nelson sees dangerous splits developing when "females are kept from claiming their assertiveness and males kept from claiming their vulnerability." Sexual violence, the macho outlook, racism, ecological damage—all express inner splits in which parts of us masquerade as our whole selves.

The way humans develop puts the important work of integrating body and spirit, sexuality and spirituality in the teenage years. Physical maturing is concrete. We can see it. Just as important is our invisible spiritual maturing—learning to make good choices, to communicate our real selves to another, to reflect on God's gifts to us, and to respond to God's call to love others. This book aims to help teens with the work of integrating sexuality and spirituality.

In talking with teens about sexuality, I hear some accuse the Church, their parents, or society of being hung up on sex, of getting bent out of shape when the subject comes up.

"Adults can hardly talk about sex without getting uptight."

"They want to take away our fun."

"They don't understand us. This is the 21st century, and things are different. They see sex as something dirty or wrong."

Probably some parents, teachers, and youth leaders feel this way. However, the vast majority of parents and adults working with youth care greatly about teens and can talk with them about what's really going on in their lives. But

good parents and adults, as well as true friends, do not always tell us what we want to hear. People who care about us will sometimes challenge us. They will point out to us when they think we are hurting ourselves or when they feel others are taking advantage of us.

When society suppressed sexuality in the 19th century, rules structured where and when men and women could meet, what kind of language they could use, and what they could wear. The Victorian dress code covered every inch of the human body more out of fear than fashion. Some of these practices treated the body and bodily functions as something intrinsically evil.

However, before we laugh at the high-collared Victorian Age, we would be wise to critique what is happening in our time. Today, an attitude too often prevails that "if it feels good, do it." The attitude assumes sex is simply a biological need that we scratch whenever it itches. This attitude follows the code, "Get as much sex as fast as you can." This *Playboy* mentality separates love, commitment, and intimacy from the sexual act. It reduces sex to a biological act that has nothing special or sacred to it. How sad that many people never get to experience sex as more.

HAVING SEX ISN'T JUST AN IMPULSE, LIKE BUYING A SHIRT OR A CANDY BAR.

Television, films, and advertising often see sex as a commodity to exploit for financial gain. Their images leave out or trivialize the love, the beauty, the work, and the value of relationships.

In such a context, the Church's view of sexuality is prophetic and counter-cultural. The Church holds that the sex act is special and sacred. The Church insists sex must be an expression of love and commitment, not something to be exploited or indulged.

Today we desperately need a balance between spirituality and sexuality. Young people, as well as all of us, need to reflect on what their sexuality means to them.

In my work, I hear the phrase casual sex. What does casual sex mean? Does it mean I had sex with someone in whom I had no investment? I really do not care about the person nor does he or she care about me. Does it mean having sex is just an impulse, like buying a shirt or a candy bar? Is it possible to have casual, throw-away sexual relationships that affect neither ourselves nor the other person? How does casual sex affect our own or the other person's self-esteem? How unimportant is casual sex if one contracts STDs or AIDS?

I ask the young people I work with, "Why not wait until you love someone and there is a mutual commitment of a marriage? Won't sex be much more fun, passionate, and fulfilling with someone who loves you as much as you love them and who is totally and faithfully committed to the relationship and to welcoming children into it?" Sex in healthy marriages is much more than casual or feel-good moments. Sex is for mutual giving to each other, not for selfish taking from each other.

How we act as sexual beings reflects who we are as spiritual beings. We express our spiritual values in our sexuality. The uniting of our spirituality and our sexually is a process, a journey. Like all journeys, this journey toward wholeness calls us to be authentic, to learn from mistakes, to travel together, and to walk with our Creator.

> **HOW WE ACT AS SEXUAL BEINGS REFLECTS WHO WE ARE AS SPIRITUAL BEINGS.**

- Identify ways people exploit sex in our society. Find and analyze examples of advertising that use sex to sell products.

- Research the Victorian period. How did people dress? What were the manners or rules of the day regarding single men and women? Plays, short stories, and parts of novels can all be helpful. Then contrast this with today's culture. What about today is better? Worse? Was the Victorian Age too artificial? Stuffy?

- What does the term casual sex mean to you?

CHAPTER 2

The Sexual Revolution: Who Won?

How did you first learn about sex? What age were you? Where did you learn?

Ask your parents and grandparents, very respectfully, how they learned about sex. What age were they? Where did they learn?

Compare how you learned about sex with how your parents and grandparents learned about sex. What was similar? What was different?

What do you think are the advantages and disadvantages to sex education today? What are advantages and disadvantages in how your parents and grandparents learned about sex?

*"Sexuality is our way of being in the world as gendered persons...
sexuality is the physiological and psychological ground of our capacity
to love."*

—*James Nelson*, The Intimate Connection*

Sociologists and sexologists trace the beginning of a sexual revolution in the United States to the period known as the Roaring Twenties. Before the 1920s sexuality was a taboo topic, rarely discussed in public. There were few books or classes on the topic.

As the sexual revolution gained momentum, sexuality slowly emerged from the closet. As early as the 1950s, some schools held one or two days of classes each year on the subject of sexuality. These classes tended to center exclusively on biology. By the late 1970s, the majority of public and private schools had expanded their health classes to include three to four days of sexuality education. Before long many schools conducted 8-, 12-, or 20-week courses on sexuality.

---

* James B. Nelson, *The Intimate Connection: Male Sexuality, Masculine Spirituality.* Louisville, Kentucky: Westminster John Knox Press, 1988.

Pioneers in the field of sexuality such as John Kinsey, Virginia Masters, and Avery Johnson studied and wrote about people's sexual feelings and practices.

Although in 1984 the covers of *Newsweek* and *Time* declared the sexual revolution dead because of AIDS, the subject of sexuality stayed out in the open. Departments concentrating on the field of human sexuality opened on university campuses. Human sexuality clinics, which treated sexual dysfunctions and problems, appeared on campuses as well as in the private sector. Couples discussed sexual issues that many of their parents or grandparents were discouraged from ever mentioning. Women, who in the past had generally been confined to the role of wife or mother, saw career options slowly open that their mothers would never have thought possible. Their changing roles in society affected their intimate relationships.

The sexual revolution also had another side. Sex became big business. American society experienced a dramatic increase in pornography in all its forms. Magazines, music, and films exploited sex for financial gain. Children as young as five began to appear in all forms of pornography. Parents sometimes sold or rented their children to pornographers who returned them to the parent(s) when they were finished. The sex industry grew as adult bookstores, adult magazines, massage parlors, strip joints, adult theaters, pimps, and prostitutes became part of the American landscape. Now cable television and the Internet beam pornography right into our homes.

- Discuss whether the sexual revolution has done more good or more harm.

- What would you want to keep from the sexual revolution? Change? Discard?

Today's adolescents have more information about sexuality at an earlier age than any generation before them. They know more at a younger age than most of their parents did. The majority of teens receive formal sexuality education by the fourth grade.

Adults who lament that times have changed are absolutely right. When they say this to adolescents, most young people shrug as if it is no big deal. Today's teens did not live in the 1940s or 1950s and cannot grasp how much the world has changed regarding sexuality. Here's an example.

I signed up as volunteer at a nursing home. An 82-year-old woman was also working at this nursing home. She was not a patient. She volunteered while still living in her own home. She helped out with patients who were sometimes younger than she. She was a wild Italian matriarch whose hands choreographed every word before she spoke it. She talked incessantly to anyone who would listen. She also got things done.

I was relaxing during a break when she plopped down next to me.

"So," she said, "I hear you talk to kids about sexuality."

I was floored. "Where did you hear that?" I managed to respond, attempting to conceal the shock I could feel forming on my face.

"Never mind," she snapped. "What do you tell them?" I looked into her face and wondered how I could answer her question without creating scandal. It is difficult to talk to one's parents about sex. This was like talking to a grandparent. I started off cautiously, not wanting to bring on cardiac arrest, but the directness of her questions showed that she could handle anything I dished out. Soon we were into the heart of it.

"I think that is great," she pronounced, slapping her hands down on the table.

"You do?" I asked in amused relief.

"Oh, yeah. These kids today are lucky. Do you want to know how I learned about sex?" she asked.

"Love to," I answered.

"I was living in Italy with my family. One of the men in our town left for America to make his fortune. He succeeded, which simply meant he secured a job and a place to live. After he was settled, he sent my family a letter requesting my older sister in marriage. My sister was 16 at the time. He also included in his letter the terms of the dowry. My parents consented, and my sister was sent on a ship to marry this man. No one asked her if she loved him. She had one escape clause. If he beat her, she could come home. He did not. And they were married.

"Six months later, my sister's husband threw a party for the new friends he had made in America. One of his friends approached my sister. He told her she was a wonderful cook, beautiful, Italian, Catholic, and were there any more like her at home? She said yes. She had a 15-year-old sister.

"He sent for me. Dowry was exchanged and I was sent to marry this man I had never laid eyes on before. I prayed all the way over on that ship that he was gentle and handsome, or at least one out of two. I arrived. We were married and my first sex class was our 'honeymoon.' I knew nothing about sex. I learned on the job. It is better today. These kids today at least know something about it. I think it is better this way."

"Whoa!" I commented. "Fifteen? That would be a freshman in high school. You would be a teen pregnancy today."

"I didn't get pregnant right away," she said softly. I was stunned.

"You didn't get pregnant right away? You weren't on birth control or..."

"Of course not," she said cutting me off with a wave of her hand. "I couldn't get pregnant. I did not have my first period until I was 16."

I don't know that a kid like this exists in present-day America. Teens today have the information. But information is not necessarily wisdom. The problems in the area of sexuality are not going away. Many are staying the same or increasing. Obviously, we need more than information. Some people believe that sexuality education is the source of many of these problems. This is simplistic thinking. These problems were around long before the first sexuality text was written. Ignorance will not eliminate these problems. It is also naïve to think that sex education can integrate information with who we are as people, our values, and our beliefs. That is the ongoing work of each young person with the help of family and mentoring Christian adults, lay or clergy.

- How would I want my own children to learn about sex? What age do I think is appropriate?

- Do I think our culture puts out too much information on sexuality, not enough, or just the right amount?

- Finish this sentence: I think the most important message about our sexuality is ...

- Get together with two or three other friends or classmates. Outline a course for fourth graders on sexuality. What would I teach in the course?

CHAPTER 3

An Intimate Faith, an Intimate God

On a scale of 1 to 5 describe your relationship with God. Let 1 mean I am very close to God; let 5 mean God is very far from me.

Describe a time you felt far away from God. Describe a time you felt close.

"There is nothing better than to be glad and to do well in life."

—*Ecclesiastes 3.12*

We who call ourselves Christians are involved in an intimate faith. When I ask teens to describe their experience of their parish liturgy on Sunday and their religious education classes, I have yet to hear a teen say, "Intimate. I find liturgy on Sunday a very intimate experience." Rather, I hear words such as "boring" and "repetitious;" and phrases such as "don't get much out of it," "seems aimed at adults," and "a lot of standing, sitting, kneeling."

16

Not all teens respond this way, of course. Many enjoy and participate enthusiastically in their liturgies and classes.

Indeed God can seem anything but intimate at times. When people close to us are ill or die, when innocent people, especially children, die from war, starvation, or disease, God can seem uncaring, aloof—a disinterested spectator. It is easy to feel this way. Many of us have.

The God of the scriptures is a feeling, caring God. I cannot really prove this. We must all discover God cares for us in the living of our lives. I do know, however, that I have watched my children, family, and friends suffer without being able to do anything for them. This does not mean I don't care.

Any of us who sincerely attempt to live by the gospel of Jesus will not leave this faith because we find it boring. Those who really live the gospel are more likely to leave because it is downright scary. Jean Donovan, and the three nuns raped and killed in El Salvador, Archbishop Oscar Romero, Dr. Thomas Dooley, Father Maximilian Kolbe, Dorothy Day, and Dr. Martin Luther King, Jr. are all people who devoted their lives, and even lost their lives, because of their love for the people they worked with and because of their love for justice. These people, as well as many others, put their lives on the line for their friends. Neither they nor their lives were boring. They followed Jesus' example. Our faith invites us to intimate, wholehearted commitment to God and God's people.

- ■ Divide into twos or threes. Research the life of one of the people mentioned above and prepare a report to the class about this person.

In my grade school years, we joked around with the phrase, "Do you know her or him in the biblical sense?" We had heard, perhaps even studied, the scripture readings from Luke 1 that Mary, the mother of Jesus, "did not know man."

"What? Was she stupid?" we asked. "There were no men in her small town? She had never met a guy before?"

No. This meant that she had not experienced sexual intercourse. I was not aware until many years later that this little joke was accurate.

The Hebrew word *yahdah* means both *to know with one's head and with one's heart*. Like the English word *know*, the word *yahdah* means *intellectual activity*, using one's head to take in the world and learn about people. *Yahdah* also means, secondly, *to have sexual intercourse*, an intimate knowing with one's heart and whole self.

The Bible uses this word that describes intimate relations between humans to describe our relationship with God. When the prophet Hosea urges the people of Israel to return to God, his poetry tells us that to know God is as possible as welcoming a sunrise.

Let us know, let us press on to know God,
Whose appearing is as sure as the dawn;
God will come to us like the showers,
Like spring rains that water the earth.

—Hosea 6.3

In creation we experience God's unconditionally loving gift of life in all its many forms. The beauty of God's creation surrounds us as reminders of this—sights, sounds, smells that cost us nothing and leave us standing in awe.

The people of Israel in their history know an intimate, personal God who reveals unconditional love for them. God is intimate to the Hebrews, close and faithful, not a God they visit for an hour on Sabbath and then completely ignore the rest of the week. The God of Israel desires a relationship, hears their cries in slavery in Egypt, and sends Moses to lead them into the desert. On their journey God makes a covenant with them: "I will be your God and you will be my people." The Ten Commandments are the terms of this covenant relationship.

The people of Israel do not view God as some distant, passive entity living in the clouds, waiting for them to decide if they believe or not. Their God actively pursues and woos them. God calls Jeremiah to be a prophet while he is still a boy. Jeremiah cannot keep from speaking God's words or they burn within him. The prophet Jonah is comic, jumping on a boat and getting swallowed by a whale as he tries to escape this God who yearns to connect with him.

Real faith is anything but boring. Faith is crazy. It is nuts. Simply scan the scriptures for evidence. "If someone strikes you on the cheek, turn your face and let him or her hit you on the other side." Right. When someone clocks me in the face, I say, "Here, I am a Christian, hit me again?" No, my first instinct is to hit the person back. "Love your enemies?" Get real. This faith is crazy. It is based on love. One of the ways I define a Christian is as a radical lover, a life giver. God loves us and calls us to love in return.

Jesus calls his disciples to love one another as he has loved them. This is his message when he celebrates Passover with them. Now, if Jesus and his disciples celebrated Passover correctly, they prepared a six- or seven-course meal, with six or seven glasses of wine. Most adults, after a huge meal with six glasses of wine

never boring.

would be ready to put their feet up, kick back, and relax. I can envision the disciples flipping on the television to watch the local soccer game or pulling out a deck of cards and starting up a poker game.

In John's story of Jesus' last supper, this beautiful, wonderful Jesus suddenly gets up on his soapbox and starts talking, telling his followers to remember this and not to forget that. He rambles on for more than four chapters in a last discourse (John 13-18). The man did not have Homiletics 101. Jesus' friends probably sat back, saying, "Jesus, slow down. Take it easy. Are you going to die tomorrow or what?" He was going to die, and they didn't know it. Jesus publicly tells 12 men, plus any others who were present, that he loves them. "As my heavenly father loves me, so do I love you...I no longer call you my servants because servants do not know what their master is about; instead I call you my friends."

Now, I don't know about the schools you attend, but at mine, if I told 12 guys, plus the others present, publicly that I loved them, I might get a reputation. This faith is crazy, and its foundation is love. The gospel message is far from boring.

- What are the basic values of the gospel of Jesus Christ?

- What are the basic values in today's American culture?

- How are the values of the gospel and American culture the same? Different?

We in the Church have often approached sexuality with more of a commandment approach than a beatitude approach. The emphasis has been on no, "Don't do this," and "Don't do that," rather than on how to appreciate and channel the sexual energy that is part of our humanity.

When I ask my students what the Church teaches about sexuality, I usually hear a chorus of don'ts. Unfortunately this is the message the Church has most

effectively conveyed to teens. Don't is one component of the Church's teaching, but there is much more.

Sexuality is aliveness. Sexuality is being a person in a body—a person who can dance and work out, a person who can shake hands and look people in the eye, a person who can embrace and communicate concern.

The love of a woman and man for each other is one image of God's love and Jesus' love for each of us. Marriage recognizes and blesses this love as a relationship that anchors many other relationships—those with family, friends, and children the couple welcomes and raises.

Sexuality is a passionate, creative, erotic energy that makes us female and male. It is a gift from God that contains not only pleasure and procreative power but also the power to express the love that two people have for each other. The clitoris of the female has one function and one function only, to pleasure. The penis of the male is very sensitive to pleasure. God created us with bodily functions that exist for pleasure as well as for procreation. This fact should reveal something to us about our Creator.

Certainly pleasure can result from the abuse of our body gifts. Sexuality can become self-centered, manipulative, and destructive when misused. When we misuse our sexuality, we cut off life. Instead of using our sexuality to make life-giving connections, we use it to manipulate and divide. We humans need to work at appreciating the sacredness in our sexuality. In our past and present, some people have viewed the body and its functions as evil and the spiritual as the only realm of good. Bodies and spirits are both the creation of God. We must reunite them.

- What messages do you receive from everyday life regarding sexuality? Are these messages positive or negative?
  Negative messages come from...
  Positive messages come from...

- What messages do you receive from the Church regarding sexuality? Which of the following statements best reflect the attitude closest to your own?

  1. *Sex is sacred and belongs totally within marriage just as the Church teaches.*

  2. *Sex is sacred and belongs mainly within marriage but not totally because sex is an important part of special relationships.*

  3. *Who I have sex with is nobody's business but mine.*

  4. *I struggle with what I know about the Church's teaching on sexuality because it's mainly what not to do. I need positive help from the Church about how to form lasting relationships.*

  5. *What does the Church know about sexuality?*

  6. *I have no idea what the Church teaches about sexuality.*

- Identify the Church's teachings that make sense to you. Identify what teachings you struggle with. Role play a conversation among a committee comprised of two teens, two parents, and one pastor about what the parish should teach middle-grade children about sexuality.

- What values will you teach?

- What restrictions will you set up?

CHAPTER 4

Two Powerful Myths About Sexuality

Those who hear my words and act on them are like the person who, in building a house, digs deep and lays a foundation on rock. When a flood arises and the river bursts against the house, it stands because it is well made.

—Luke 6.47-4

Take the Sexual Myth Test below. Answer true or false. When you finish, compare your answers with the correct answers on page 126. Then tally as a class how many got perfect scores, how many got 11-14 correct, and how many got 6-10 correct.

1. The male penis only becomes erect during lovemaking or while the male is thinking of sexual activity.

2. A woman cannot get pregnant before she has her first period.

3. Teens have the highest rate of STDs (sexually transmitted diseases).

4. STDs can result in a baby being born blind.

5. Orgasm is the peak or climax of sexual activity.

6. Sexual intercourse the night before or the day of athletic competition will reduce excellence in athletic performance.

7. Women have a larger epididymis than men.

8. Sexual intercourse should be avoided during pregnancy.

9. A large penis enhances a woman's sexual gratification.

10. Masturbation is a sexual activity common to both men and women.

11. *The majority of sexually transmitted diseases will go away by themselves.*

12. *Most teen mothers do not complete high school or acquire employment skills and are likely to end up on welfare.*

13. *After two or three birth control pills, a woman can no longer get pregnant.*

14. *The absence of a hymen is positive evidence that a girl is not a virgin.*

15. *There is an absolute, safe period for sexual intercourse during which conception will not take place.*

■ Share any sexual myths you remember from growing up, for example, the stork bringing babies. Share any current myths you have heard in school, at parties, from friends.

Myths about sexuality are global and plentiful. They masquerade as facts: A woman cannot get pregnant the first time she has sex. The buildup of sperm in the male body will cause acne.

Every generation seems to have its own myths about sexuality. This chapter will highlight two myths that are attitudinal. They exist in varying degrees of severity.

The first myth is that we are not able to talk about sexuality.

The second myth is that we are supposed to know everything about sexuality.

Let's start with an explanation of the first myth: We are not supposed to talk about sexuality. I can still hear teachers telling me, "Hey, if you are a Christian man or woman, you will never discuss that topic, not in mixed company. Okay, maybe once in a while in the locker room, but that is it." Or, "Hey, I do not want to hear those kinds of dirty jokes." The don't-talk-about-it myth is often strong in families. Sexuality is not always the most comfortable topic for parents and teens to talk about. Most families do not get up in the morning, mom and dad getting ready for

Myths masqu

work, the kids getting ready for school, and amid the Wheaties, Grape Nuts, and toast, the kids inquire, "Hey, Mom and Dad, how's your sex life going? Is it going pretty good? Well, that's great."

In my family someone would have died at the breakfast table. Probably me. One of my parents would have taken the box of cereal and jammed it down my throat. I would have gone to school with a big bulge in my neck.

"Bartlett, what's that thing sticking out your neck?" my friend asks me. But before I can answer, he says, "You brought up sex again at breakfast, didn't you? No explanation is necessary. I understand."

Sexuality is personal. Most of us do not hop on a bus, turn to the person next to us, and ask how his or her sex life is going. Most of us would not or should not discuss sexuality freely without trusting the other person. But when we meet someone we care about and want to be in relationship with, it is critical that we can talk to him or her.

It is sad to work with teens, as well as adults, who engage in sexual behavior with each other but cannot talk about sexuality. This is a definite signal that something is amiss. This is not healthy. We need to be able to share what is comfortable and uncomfortable about our sexuality. Often when I bring this topic up, some teens claim that only up-tight adults have problems talking about sex. Teens have no problems discussing sexuality. Not always true. I often hear from teens who have a hard time communicating on this topic. Here is an example.

rade as facts.

This was their third date. He was falling more and more in love. But he was male. He was cool. He wasn't going to say, "I love you more than anyone I've ever met. All I can think of is you." No. All of these feelings translate into, "I had a good time tonight." He steals a glance at the digital clock in the car. She has to be home in a half hour. He is five minutes from her house. He has time. This is the night to find out if there is hope, if she feels what he feels, if this is more than a friendship. He eases the car into a dark, romantic spot, turns off the 537 horsepower, and gazes into her eyes.

"Let's talk," he whispers. Talk is the last thing on his mind. They talk for a good 40 seconds. Then he begins to raise his arm in the direction of her shoulder. When the arm lands softly onto her shoulder, there are two possibilities. She may fly to the passenger's side of the seat and scream, "Get your hands off me. Touch me again, and I'll rip you face off!" Or, she will smile and snuggle up closer.

As his arm slowly descends onto her shoulder, she moves closer to him. Immediately his mind races with the words, "Yes! She does like me! We are more than friends!" Tonight he imagines will be a peak experience for him. He turns to kiss her. She leans to receive the embrace, placing her hand on the seat.

As he moves closer, he pushes the seat belt buckle onto her hand and before she can move it, he sits on the buckle, pinning her hand beneath it. She cannot move it. Pain shoots all the way up her shoulder. She can take her pulse without touching her wrist or neck. She can just feel the throbbing one...two...three.... He notices she is trembling and is glad to see she is just as excited as he is. Finally her arm goes numb and she cannot feel anything.

After what seems an eternity, he pulls away and tells her, "I better get you home." She nods and thanks God that her hand, though numb, is now free. He pulls into her driveway and escorts her to the door.

"I'll call you," he promises.

"Please do," she replies, as she slowly moves into the house. She waves to him, shuts the door, and grabs her hand.

"My hand!" she moans as she massages it with the other. "My hand! I am

going to lose my hand." She notices that the letters GM are imprinted solidly into the back of her hand. The next morning the letters remain. Nothing she does will take them away. Friends at school ask why she has GM indented into the back of her hand. "Ah....the concert last night." She explains. "There was this huge guy stamping people at the gate and he just stamped so hard, it's still there," she says with a weak smile.

This example illustrates the don't-talk myth in action. It takes this guy three dates to make a move. The girl doesn't want to ruin this romantic moment by blurting out, "You're sitting on my hand, and it hurts." She just endures. She just goes along, fakes it. The example shows how crazy this myth is.

Men are just as guilty as women of not communicating. For example, some males will go out with a female, enjoy being with her, and find her easy to talk with. But when the guys are around, they will suddenly act distant and cool. They don't want their friends to discover that they really like a girl for fear of getting mocked about "the wife" or being "whipped." Their tough or aloof act confuses or even hurts the girl. These guys resist talking to the girl or their friends about how they really feel.

The don't-talk pattern can be harmful when adults carry it into their relationships and marriages. For many adults who are incapable of talking about their sexuality, these patterns begin to take root in junior and senior high.

When two people are going further physically than they are verbally, this is often a warning sign that something could be wrong in the relationship. Communication about sexuality is necessary in a healthy relationship.

The inability to communicate about sexuality can be carried into adult relationships. A woman I once counseled complained of not feeling safe dressing in the morning with her husband present. She dressed inside her closet so that her husband did not see her and suddenly want to be sexual. She was not

27

comfortable telling him that his response to seeing her getting dressed was building up feelings of resentment in her.

Husbands often complain to one another that they and their wives have too little time for each other and not enough time for sex. "My wife is always so busy and the kids come first." But these husbands hesitate to talk about their feelings with their wives. Communication between people in sexual relationships is vital.

- What examples of people having trouble communicating about sex have you heard? Why is it difficult to talk about sex at times?

- Do you find it more difficult to talk about sexual matters with people of the same sex or the opposite sex? Why?

The second myth is that we are supposed to know everything about sex and sexuality. This myth assumes that at some moment a bright light appears in the sky and descends upon a child. There are voices. Instantly she or he knows everything about sex. The child walks into the house, summons the family around, and announces, "Mom, Dad, my darling sister and brother, I just want you to know that if any of you have any questions about sex, feel free to come to me. Don't be embarrassed. No question is too stupid. My door is always open. Anything you want to talk about, feel free. I will always be there for you." This doesn't happen. None of us knows everything about sex, but most of us fear getting caught not knowing.

If you are at a party and someone cracks a political joke about the lieutenant governor, you simply say you don't get it.

"Who is the lieutenant governor?" You ask. "Oh, Smith. Oh, now I get it." But if someone cracks a joke about sexuality, people nervously look at each other for two, three seconds before bursting into fake laughter. Then you motion to your friend and ask, "What does orgasm mean?"

"I don't know," your friend says. "Go look it up."

There is pressure on us to know everything about sexuality. This pressure can be overwhelming.

My friend's brother was getting married. He was 23, a plumber. I was invited to the stag party a week before the wedding. The groom-to-be came over to talk to three of us whom he must have felt safe with.

"I got to tell you guys something," he said, lowering his voice, the smell of liquor on his breath. "I'm a virgin."

One of my friends looked at him incredulously. "But you told me back in high school that you did it with..."

"I know," he said, interrupting him. "I told a lot of stories. I didn't want anyone to think I was weird. But the truth is, I was a virgin. But I just lost my virginity."

"Just now, did I miss something?" another friend joked.

The groom-to-be waved him off with his hand, "No, not here, you idiot. Saturday."

"Oh, you and your fiancée had sex?" the friend asked.

"No," he replied. "Not with her." Now all of us were curious.

I said, "Let me get this straight. You waited 23 years to have sex. Then a week before your marriage you had sex, and it wasn't with your fiancée. Who did you have it with?"

A sheepish grin crawled on his face. "I went into Chicago and hired a prostitute. Hey, I didn't want to go on my honeymoon and not know what I was doing. She's a virgin, too, at least she says she is. Heck, one of us has to know what we're doing."

"Well," my friend commented, "I bet if you had waited, you two would have figured it out. I mean, if you go to the right honeymoon places they have instructions written right on the inside of the medicine cabinet. You can just open it up and follow the diagrams."

We were making jokes but actually all of us thought this was a pretty sorry story. It is an example of how much pressure in our culture there is to know about sex. We actually felt sorry for this guy. He put sex off all of these years only to do it first with someone he did not care about and who didn't care about him. What a waste!

> **THOSE WHO ACT AS IF THEY KNOW EVERYTHING OFTEN KNOW THE LEAST.**

The groom-to-be waited over a year before he told his wife this story. He thought she would be angry; he was surprised to discover it saddened her. She could not understand. She told him they had an entire lifetime together to "get it right." She told him how special that would have been to her. The pressure to know all about sexuality can be strong.

The reality is that none of us know everything and we never will. We will learn about sexuality throughout our lifetime. We will learn things at 16, 17, 20, 30, 40, 50, 80.

Once, when I said this in a class I was teaching, one freshman looked up and remarked, "Eighty! Why bother?" I smiled, approached the desk of this student, and asked if he had eaten lunch.

"Yeah, why?" he responded.

"Good." I answered, "Is it disturbing to think of your parents being sexual?"

"Gross," he shot back.

I quietly suggested, "Well, then think of your grandparents having sex." He

30

immediately slipped into a catatonic state! It took two days for his coach and me to finally get him moving and to basketball practice!

We learn about sexuality our entire lives. Age does not matter. Sexuality is us as body persons on a lifelong journey of interrelatedness with others, especially our partners in marriage. The sooner we can admit we do not know everything and never will, the healthier our sexuality will be. Often the people who act as if they know everything, know the least. The students who can ask questions, who are brave enough to say they are not sure what that word means, are usually the healthy ones. I personally believe that it is refreshing to know that we can learn about sexuality our entire lives.

- What pressure do you experience to know all about sexuality? What pressure did you feel when you were younger?

- With whom do you find it difficult or easy to talk about sexuality?

- How easy or difficult in your family is talking about sex?

- If you have dated, how easy or difficult do you find it to talk to the other person about sex?

- If you haven't dated, how easy or difficult do you think it will be to talk to the other person about sex?

CHAPTER 5

Intimacy with Our Bodies and Ourselves

On a scale of 1 to 5 rate how you like yourself. Let 1 mean not at all; let 5 mean very much.

What two things you would magically change about your appearance and personality, if you could?

What two things would you never want to lose about your appearance and personality?

Which was easier to identify, qualities you would change or qualities you would keep?

"Too often we attempt to control young people's use of their sexual faculties, instead of helping them to get to the point where self-control is an outgrowth of their self-esteem. To do this we must be adults who show them how to love themselves so they can love (and not use) their neighbors."

—Paul Dinter, "Getting Some Respect."*

* Paul Dinter, "Getting Some Respect," *Church*. February, 1987.

The scene in the gospels where a scribe asks Jesus which is the greatest of the commandments is an enlightening story. In Matthew's gospel, Jesus replies, "You shall love the Lord your God with your whole heart, with your whole soul, and with all your mind. This is the greatest and first commandment. The second is like it: You shall love your neighbor as yourself. On these two commandments the whole law is based, and the prophets as well (Matthew 22.37-40)." We all have heard these words, but seldom do we personally feel the immense power they contain.

Jesus tells us to love God, our neighbor, and ourselves. For our faith to be holistic we need to love all three. Many of the teens I work with struggle with loving themselves, with accepting who they are.

In order to have a healthy sexuality we must be able to appreciate and care about ourselves. If we do not value ourselves, it is difficult to value others. If we do not value and care about our own bodies, we most likely will not value or care about the bodies of others. If any of us have friends who trash or do not take care of their own CD player or DVDs, we would naturally hesitate to let them borrow ours. It is the same principle.

Most of us do not go Christmas shopping for a brother, sister, parent, or close friend and intentionally choose something he or she will hate. We do not purchase an especially ugly and useless item, carefully wrap it, and give it to a special person as a gift. We do not watch as he or she excitedly rips open the present, only to discover, "I hate this. Do you have the receipt?"

As stupid as this sounds, that is exactly what we are doing in relationships when we do not value ourselves. We are giving a gift to people that we are convinced they will not like.

In counseling sessions with teens and adults, I often work with people who are not in healthy relationships. These people will compromise themselves, their values, and their beliefs in order to get other people to like them. They will gossip about good friends to impress someone or get on his or her good side. They will betray the confidences of close friends in order to look important to someone else they want to like them. They will smoke cigarettes to fit in. They will use alcohol and drugs to gain acceptance. They will shoplift as a shortcut to popularity.

People will have sex with others to gain their approval. Some will completely cut off family and friends, isolating themselves just to be with someone they think loves them. All of these patterns can result in pain, loneliness, and varying degrees of self-destructiveness.

We must first valu

People with healthy self-images can do these things as well. However, as a counselor I find that the people who do value themselves usually recognize destructive patterns earlier and recover more quickly. They can more readily admit they made a mistake. Those who care little for themselves struggle longer to break these harmful patterns and are more likely to repeat them. A healthy self-esteem increases one's chance of a healthy sexuality.

One young woman I worked with had a number of sexual encounters at an early age. Her self-esteem was poor. Every guy she went out with was a guy she ended up having sex with. As I got to know her better it became clear to her and me that she did not believe a guy would like her unless she had sex with him. She just did not believe that she was worth loving, or that guys could love her unless she gave them what they wanted.

This has become a deep, destructive pattern. Her relationships have turned increasingly violent and abusive. The men she dates control her life. They have sex when they please. They hit her or physically threaten her if she does not do exactly what they want her to do. She is verbally or physically abused if she talks to any other guys, whether they are just friends or not. At one point she articulated, "No guy will stay with me unless I give him what he wants." But even her own realization has not been enough to stop her destructive pattern.

I have challenged her to go out with a guy, get to know him, and have fun without getting sexual. I have implored her to connect with female friends and just drop males for the time being.

At present, she has not been able to do this, even though she wants to. Her pattern runs deep and will not die easily. This girl is pretty, she is smart, she is fun to be around, but at this time in her life she is incapable of believing this about herself. She does not believe she is worthwhile. When others treat her as if she is worthless, they confirm her own feeling. This has become a vicious cycle in her life. In recognizing the pattern, she has taken the first step to changing it and has a reason for hope.

 ourselves.

All of us have to be able to look in the mirror and accept who we are. The book of Genesis tells us that we are made "in the image and likeness of God." We have a hard time believing this. What a powerful statement this is if we can begin to grasp it!

If we want to know what God looks like, we can look around our class, school, team, neighborhood, and church. The faces we see are what God looks like. This is the closest we are going to get to seeing God, unless we have a vision. We are all created in the image and likeness of God. This means that each and every one of us is sacred and precious. We need to accept ourselves and our bodies. We need to look in that mirror and say that we are attractive and handsome, that we are okay. This is the initial step towards a healthy sexuality.

Once I was working with a woman in her 40s who was attractive but did not believe it. Her assignment, after one of our sessions, was to go home, gaze into her mirror, and say that she was okay, that she was attractive. For three weeks she was unable to do this. One day she came to a session and proudly announced that she had done her homework. I had forgotten.

"What homework?" I inquired.

"The mirror," she answered.

I was pumped. "You looked into the mirror and said you were attractive? You looked into your eyes and said it?" I asked happily.

Her smile left. "You didn't say I had to look into my eyes."

"Wait. You mean you looked down?" I asked. She nodded. "I want you to go home to that mirror, look yourself in the eyes, and say you are attractive," I said. It took her another two weeks before she could do this. I hope that all of us are able to do this well before our 40s.

■ **Work with a partner or a small group to express differences between a healthy self-image and conceit.**

Some teens feel that to appreciate and like themselves is conceited. There is a difference between conceit and self-esteem. It is healthy to feel good about one's self. People with healthy self-images do not need to tell everyone how great they are because they generally feel secure with themselves. If I am struggling to accept myself, I am more likely constantly to remind everyone else how great I am because I feel insecure with myself. Feeling good about one's self will diminish conceitedness.

As simple as all of this may sound, it is not easy. We live in a culture that bombards us with what perfect people and bodies should look like. This is especially true for adolescents.

Guys see athletes in ads who ripple with just-do-it muscles that make them feel too thin or short or flabby to try out for school teams. They see clothing ads in which the men turn an indifferent shoulder to the world, modeling distance rather than closeness in relationships. Girls and boys see faces airbrushed, soft-lighted, acne-free. Young men and women see ads in magazines for teens that picture sexual activity as fashionable and sell jeans by picturing them being taken off. Black girls must watch perfect bouncing hair swirl on the tube, unlike the tight curl in their own.

We can hardly open a magazine, turn on the television, or watch a movie without images reminding all of us how we don't quite measure up. There is defense in recognizing that advertising puts us down for a reason—to set us up for buying products that improve us.

We need to recognize the women and men who appear in ads are nauseatingly perfect. Once in a while an old person sells dentures or laxatives, but this is rare. Usually we see perfect people, so perfect that if we look closely they actually look somewhat phony or mannequin-like. Scrutiny of a magazine photo reveals that these people have no flaws, no blemishes; in fact they do not even have pores. They have been airbrushed out. Few of us stop to think that these models have been in make-up for three hours before the shoot. Most of us would probably look decent after three hours of make-up. More and more people today know how easily airbrushes and computer enhancement make people look thinner, tanner, younger. Beauty salons offer special packages that fit a customer's face into various new hair styles and cuts—a fun way to get a look at a new do.

A deeper defense against the message of advertising is recognizing how beautiful people look when they are excited or in love. We often look at ourselves in the mirror more as an object. We don't see ourselves the way others see us—alive and unselfconscious. Andre Agassi reminds us, "Image is

everything," but some of us are still naive enough to believe that substance counts. Who we are is much more than we see.

Former and present beauty contestants reveal that they and their competitors tape up their breasts and hips to firm up and accentuate these parts of their bodies. They spread Vaseline on their teeth to shine in the lights. Some contestants pay for liposuction or cosmetic surgery to improve parts of their bodies. Some women, because they are born with shorter or larger bodies or because they have larger bone structures, never have a chance in these contests.

Advertising promotes a narrow definition of beauty in our culture.

As young women dream about resembling these illusionary people, we often are unaware of what goes on behind the glitter. Cher, Gretchen Carlson (former Miss America), Jane Fonda, Christie Brinkley, all within a year of each other, shared their struggles with anorexia and bulimia as they tried to keep their perfect bodies.

The perfect image can become an obsession. On some retreats, breakfast time is set at 8:30 A.M. and leaders discover young women up at 6:30 or earlier, getting ready. The number of junior and senior high girls who use diet pills and starve themselves so they will look right is increasing. Eating disorders are also occurring at younger ages. Dr. Jean Kilbourne, in her excellent documentary, "Still Killing Us Softly," points to a survey done among fourth-grade students. Over half of the girls who answered the survey felt they needed to go on a diet. Kilbourne reports that over $10 million an hour is spent on cosmetic products in this country alone. We get obsessed with our bodies.

MYTH

IMAGE IS
EVERYTHING!

The obsession with bodies includes males. The National Institute on Drug Abuse (NIDA) estimates a half million high school boys take steroids. In 2001, the NIDA surveyed about 44,000 students from 424 secondary schools across the United States. They found that steroid use among seniors rose from 1.7% to 2.4% in 2000, despite its side effects such as "backne" and "roid rage." Home-run slugger Mark McGwire used androstenedione, a steroid hormone allowed in professional baseball but banned in other sports. In a survey NBC asked Olympic athletes, "If we invented a steroid that would improve your athletic performance by 50%, but would kill you in four years, would you use it?" Over half the respondents said yes. This is how compulsive we can get about our bodies. The media does not deserve the entire blame for our obsession with body image, but they contribute to it.

- What evidence of too much stress on looks do you experience in our culture? Do you feel there is more pressure on women, on men, or equal pressure on both?

- What body image stereotypes do you think especially hurt young people of your gender and race?

- When have you caught yourself judging people on their looks before getting to know them?

- How important is personality to you in dating? Do women place greater importance on personality than men or vice versa?

- If you were offered a drug or untraceable steroid that would make you one of the top athletes in your school but would cause sickness and possible death by age 25, how tempted would you be to use it? What if other team members used it? Would these choices put more pressure on you?

- Role play a situation in which a depressed young person, a boy or girl, confides to two friends that he or she feels worthless and just does not like who he or she is. Have three people volunteer to role play, and have others observe and evaluate what they dislike and like about how the two respond. Other groups of three can role play the same situation to explore other possible responses.

There is nothing wrong with wanting to lose some weight or look better. All of us feel short-changed at times. Sometimes we wish we were taller, smaller, thinner, bigger. We want brown eyes, green eyes, better teeth, thicker hair. Such wishing can become dangerous if it turns compulsive.

MYTH

YOU CAN NEVER BE TOO THIN.

We have to learn to live with and accept the bodies we were given. Every one of us has unique abilities and talents that no one else has. We have to accept ourselves as body people, embodied spirits. One of the subtle goals of advertising is to create the feeling that we who see the ads are somehow incomplete. We will be better off, feel more complete, if we purchase their product. The gospel message of Jesus is just the opposite. We are good not because of what we do or own, not because of our looks, but because we are a creation of God.

- Describe what makes a fun date for you. What is the person you are dating like? What are the three top qualities you look for in a date?

- Read Matthew 6.25-34 as a prayer. Do you believe this reading? What gets in the way of believing this reading?

The Wonder and the Power of Touch.

How many people
touch you in a day?
How many of these
are the same sex?
Opposite sex?
What kind of touch
do you like?
Dislike?

*"Blessed are those who give me a hug when
I need it most."*

*"Blessed are those who cuddle when
I cuddle."*

—*Sexuality beatitudes*
from high school students

Almost everyone that Jesus healed he touched. There are a few exceptions.

He heals the Roman centurion's servant from a distance without touching him.

But in most other cases, Jesus touches the people he heals.

42

Touch is a powerful human resource. One gospel story that brings out the power of touch is Luke 8.40-49. In this scene a woman with a hemorrhage touches the tassel of Jesus' cloak. Immediately Jesus asks who touched him. His disciples tell him it could have been anyone in the crowd surrounding them, but Jesus insists, "Someone touched me; I know that power has gone forth from me." Touch conveys energy. It has tremendous power to heal, to comfort, to provide pleasure.

Touch also has the capacity to tear down and destroy. That is why touch that is hurtful or abusive can be so damaging to people. Father Val Peters, the director of Boys and Girls Town, says that the bumper sticker "Have you hugged your child today?" does not apply to the young people at Boys Town. Most of the young men and women there are working at building personal boundaries they never developed because they experienced various kinds of abuse. For them it is important not to be touched in any way unless they give permission. We humans possess the power to use touch in positive or negative ways.

Touch is one of the life-giving, primal forces in nature as well as in human nature. My sister-in-law bought a designer dog, a $200 puppy with more papers than any of our three children. She paid for the dog, but the kennel said she must wait six weeks to bring the puppy home. After four weeks, she was too excited to wait longer and went to get the dog. The breeder refused to let her take the puppy and insisted that it remain with its mother for the entire six weeks to complete the bonding process. The breeder could not guarantee that

the puppy would be normal if my sister-in-law took the dog any earlier. The breeder explained that when she had let the puppies go earlier in the past, their behavior became neurotic. They acted strange, seemed confused about sexual identity, and were more difficult to house break. Puppies need a mother

dog's touch—being cuddled, caressed, played with, licked, nuzzled—or they will be emotionally disturbed, psychologically disturbed, or even die.

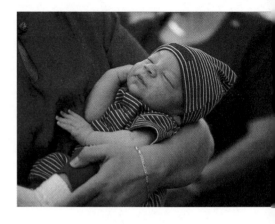

Human babies do not survive or thrive without touch. The iron crib babies of Romania serve as a recent example. Orphanages placed babies three or four to a metal crib, cattled together in pens. The doctors who came to these orphanages after the fall of the Romanian government reported that these children were physically smaller than other children of their age. They discovered that they lagged behind in social and intellectual development. Some were mentally or physically retarded.

How had this happened? One of the reasons for the children's condition was the lack of human touch. These babies were fed without being held. When they cried, no one held them or comforted them. They were deprived of human contact. They were also malnourished and lived in their excrement sometimes for several days.

A famous psychology experiment compares how touch affects the growth of three baby monkeys. The real mother feeds one monkey. The second monkey draws milk from a bottle placed in towel; the third gets milk from a bottle placed in a wire frame. The third monkey dies. The first thrives far more than the second. Touch is as necessary as food in the growth of animals and humans.

ALL HUMAN BEINGS REQUIRE NURTURING TOUCH.

The *New York Times* conducted a study in the 1970s in which they inter-viewed 100 inmates on Death Row. All of the inmates were male. All of them had killed one or more people. The researchers were trying to determine if these men had things in common. They found that of the 100 men they interviewed, 72 had experienced physical or sexual abuse growing up.

People can die from a lack of human affection and intimacy. One illustration of this is the film, "Cipher in the Snow." The film is a true story about a sixth-grade boy. The boy gets sick on the bus, asks the bus driver to pull over, stumbles to the open bus door, and collapses into a snow bank. The driver radios for emergency help. The paramedics pronounce the boy dead when they arrive. The autopsy reveals that there is no physical cause to explain the boy's death.

At the request of the hospital staff, the school investigates why the boy died. A math teacher heads up the investigation and discovers that the boy's mother divorced and remarried. The stepfather verbally and physically abused the boy and told the mother not to baby him with touch or affection. The boy grew progressively isolated and withdrawn from the hurt of the world.

The investigation concludes the boy died from a broken heart. His body quit functioning. He lost his will to go on and just stopped living. In 1978, a college woman found dead in her dormitory room in Winona, Minnesota, was also listed as having died from similar causes.

TOUCH IS A POWERFUL HUMAN RESOURCE.

Touch can help heal neglected children. When I was working in a parish, I witnessed in a child-neglect case both the negative effects of lack of touch and the positive effects of an adoptive family's love.

Two young neighbors discovered the eight-month-old baby girl when they heard her crying on a Friday evening. The parents had gone to their cabin and left the child alone for the weekend. One of the neighbors was in my youth group and called me that night, saying she had an emergency. The baby was taken to the hospital. Her name was Amy.

When I first saw this baby, the child had black and blue marks on its neck, shoulders, and arms. The doctor explained that this was not from abuse but neglect. She said when parents bring home a baby, hold it, play with it, tickle it, bathe it, they are doing the baby a favor. Touch stimulates blood flow.

This is the same principle at work in treating frostbite. If you are out skiing and notice a white spot on your friend's nose or cheek, the first thing to do is put your hand on the area. Don't rub it or you will rub the skin off. The warmth of your hand will stimulate blood flow.

The doctor estimated the parents held this baby no more than once or twice a day. She was not receiving normal stimulation. The doctor explained that if she were to take ultra-sounds of the veins and arteries of a two-week-old baby and the veins and arteries of this eight-month-old girl, the pictures would look identical. This little infant girl's body was not working to full capacity. As a result, if Amy was playing in her crib and bumped her arm against the crib, she bruised very easily. Her everyday movements caused broken blood vessels. She also was suffering from malnourishment, which made her skin lighter and heightened the visibility of the bruises.

When her family returned from the cabin, a neighbor told them that Amy was in the hospital. The family had to go to court to get her back. After four days in court, the family skipped town without Amy. The court placed Amy in a foster home and later put her up for adoption. The adoption agency sought to place her with what they referred to as a high-touch family. It was the first time I had ever heard this expression.

Amy was placed, and for the first six years of her life was emotionally disturbed. Any kind of touch terrified her. A new babysitter could recognize Amy's emotional problems as easily as a psychiatrist. If her adoptive parents left a new babysitter momentarily alone with Amy and the sitter decided to join her on the floor but in doing so surprised her with a touch, Amy might freak out, shaking as if she were having seizures.

Amy did not do this all the time, even when someone she didn't know surprised her. But sometimes she did. When Amy was two, she was playing with some neighbor children. One came up and grabbed her from behind. Amy told the child to let her go. When he did not, Amy whirled on him, scratching and biting his face. The child went home crying. The mother came over to show Amy's mother what Amy had done to her child. Her mom began searching for Amy. Fifteen minutes later she found her in a closet curled up in the fetal position, just shaking.

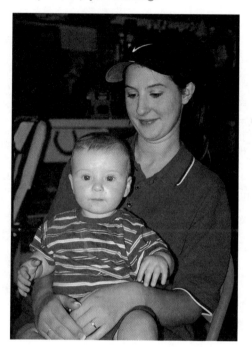

When Amy went to preschool, someone in the family had to go with her and hold her for up to an hour before she felt safe in joining the other children. This went on for two months. Amy is now in her teens and doing quite well, primarily because of the love her adopted family has given her. Her case illustrates dramatically that how we are touched, held, and cuddled is important to who we are and to our sexuality.

- Talk with your parents about how you responded to various kinds of touch as a child.

- Find articles on the iron crib babies of Romania, or any recent local articles concerning abuse or neglect.

- Bring in a doctor or nurse who works in pediatrics to talk about the role of touch in the lives of infants and children.

CHAPTER 7

Bonding

Provide the people in your group each an orange and give them five minutes to get to know their orange, to handle it, look at it, smell it, discover its special features, and name it. Have each group member introduce his or her orange. Ask how many in your group want to exchange oranges at the end of this time.

"Sexuality is a fundamental component of personality, one of its modes of being, of manifestation, of communicating with others, of feeling, of expressing, and of living human love."

—The Truth and Meaning of Human Sexuality #10

---

* The Pontifical Council for the Family, *The Truth and Meaning of Human Sexuality* #10, 1995.

If you felt you wanted to keep your orange, you experienced bonding, a natural process we all experience. Human bonding takes far longer than the five minutes with an orange or the six weeks puppies need with their mothers. The process is longer and more complex.

For the first nine months of our lives, we humans live in a wonderful place—the womb. The womb has a heated swimming pool in which we can just lie back and relax. The lighting is never too bright or too dark. The umbilical cord pipes food directly into our stomachs. We do not have to worry about how it tastes or about chewing it.

The womb is climate controlled, no heat waves or cold snaps to contend with. The womb provides transportation. Wherever mom goes, we follow. If mom does some aerobics or running, we get bumped around and get some exercise.

After about nine months, earthquakes begin to rock paradise. These earthquakes become more frequent and more severe. This is not an easy time or vacation. The hard work both the mother and child must do give birthing the name labor. This process can last anywhere from a coveted 30 minutes to a less desirable, 2, 10, 20, 40, 60 hours.

Labor begins with the water in the mother's womb breaking. Suddenly we find the pool emptying and wonder what is happening. "Fine. If someone has to clean the pool, it's okay. Clean the pool, but fill it back up. I like the water."

Then we find ourselves being forced out a small opening, whether we like it or not. Our mothers push. A total stranger pulls us out but doesn't say, "Hey, you have been through quite an ordeal. Here, have a Coke." No, the stranger slaps us on the rear, even though we did nothing wrong and assigns us to a nursery full of total strangers without taking time for any introductions.

So we scream—that's birth. More accurately, that was birth, my birth.

Presently, parents, doctors, and nurses work to make birth a welcome into the family and into the world. Today couples have the option of attending prenatal classes together. These classes serve to prepare the parents for the birth experience and instruct them on relaxing and breathing techniques which can be helpful during the birth process. These methods also serve to jumpstart the bonding process of child with parent.

CHILDBIRTH IS A HOLY AND WONDERFUL MOMENT TO LOOK FORWARD TO AS A MARRIED COUPLE.

Couples can choose the sort of birth experience they want for themselves and their child. Some couples choose to have the birth in the comfort of their home with the assistance of a midwife. The Lamaze birth process uses relaxation and breathing to ease the mother's fear and pain and the baby's entry into the world. Often the doctor or midwife takes the baby from the birth canal and places the newborn child directly onto the warmth and flesh of the mother's stomach. Today doctors and midwives encourage fathers to be in the birthing room and take an active role in the labor and birth of their child. When I was born, my father was not allowed in the birthing room, but I had the privilege of being present for the births of all three of my children.

These were experiences that I will never forget. I was afraid I might faint, but once the birth process began, I was so fascinated by what was taking place that these fears never entered my mind. They were truly miraculous experiences. I felt so close, so bonded with my wife as she struggled through this process.

Since then, I have always wanted to make it mandatory for every high school male to watch a woman go through labor and delivery. First, I think many males would think long and hard about having sex when they realize the labor a woman must go through to bring a child into the world. Second, males would realize the importance of welcoming a child into a family that is ready to care for him or her. However, many women, even with a one-way window, would not be comfortable with a class full of high school students watching them give birth. This is a holy and wonderful moment to look forward to as a married couple.

- What do you know about your own birth? How long was it? What were the circumstances? Who was present? If you are adopted, what do you know about the adoption? If you can't answer these questions, ask your parents.

- What method of birth would you choose?

- Invite a midwife, nurse, doctor, or parent to come in and talk about what the birth process is like. Also invite them to share the advantages and disadvantages they see in the birthing options. What changes have they witnessed in the birthing process?

Psychologists point out that for the first year and a half of our lives, we live in an extension of the womb—the family. We are no longer inside our mothers' bodies, but moms and dads surround and protect us with care. They feed us, change the diapers, put us to sleep.

We do not see infants and toddlers taking charge of their families. "Hey, Mom, Dad, you look tired. Sit down. I'll make dinner tonight. We'll have some of these Gerber's peaches, and these rude-looking green beans you have been forcing down my throat. Now you can find out what they taste like."

No. Parents take care of the kids. Babies very gradually begin to realize that there is a bigger world out there. Parents belong to this bigger world and so do brothers, sisters, grandparents, friends, babysitters. After the age of two, children reach out more curiously to connect with this bigger world. They begin to break out of their psychological womb. Some will do this quickly; others slowly. Abandonment, neglect, and abuse can destroy the security a child needs to venture out into this outer world.

At two, children don't pack up their suitcases, say goodbye, and come back at three all grown up. But they enter a new phase in the bonding process and begin stretching the bonds with mom and dad. Many people call this age the "terrible twos." Suddenly the cute little baby who is learning to talk and walk turns into a raging brat. New parents frantically dial up their counselors, doctors, or friends to report their child is out of control. "What's wrong? I had this wonderful, fun kid, and suddenly he or she has had this complete personality change. The kid is so stubborn. My child won't let me or anyone help with anything. The kid insists on doing everything for himself or herself." These parents have an entirely normal child. Beginning at the age of two or three, kids start to exert their independence.

Here is a typical scene in a family with a terrible two-year-old. The parent is preparing breakfast in the morning.

Sex is sacred.

"I want to pour the cereal," the child declares.

The parent calmly says, "No. Yesterday you poured an entire box of Cheerios on the table and the floor. We are still crunching them with our bare feet. Today I will help you."

After a 10-minute battle the parent wins and pours the cereal. The child quietly slips off to grab the milk jug, which weighs more than the child. The parent dives for the falling milk carton, rescuing half of the contents, while the other half turns the kitchen floor into a white lake.

This same child will insist on picking out his or her own clothes, creating colorful combinations he or she will not wear again until college. These children are exerting independence as they begin the work of emerging from the family womb.

Another marvelous ritual of the terrible twos is the chanting of the word mine.

"That's mine, mine, mine!"

"Alicea, please share your blocks with Damon."

"No, they're mine!"

A child of two does wonderful, touching things, too. He or she ventures out to the backyard and gathers together a bouquet of dandelions for the parent. Mom or Dad receives them, places them in a vase, and perhaps feels tears welling up. The dandelions are of no value. What makes dandelion bouquets so special to parents is the child reaching out and giving something back, a refreshing respite from the constant taking.

I can hear teens respectfully grumbling, "So we bond at two or three. Who cares?" At this early age, the child is reaching out to this larger world for the first time. The child does this by reaching out to parents, siblings, and significant people. Most people are good enough parents, so a child bonds and learns to trust the world. However, abuse or neglect can cause children to distrust people and the world around them. If a child wakes at two o'clock in the morning crying because of hunger or discomfort and no one comes, the child can experience the world as an uncaring, unsafe place. This is especially true if this is not a one-time occurrence but happens frequently. Such neglect can diminish the child's self-esteem and cause emotional, psychological, or even physical harm, as in the cases of the iron crib babies.

Childhood bonding experiences with family and friends are incredibly life giving. Families and friends encircle most children with deep love.

My wife, Anne Marie, and I attended a Christmas party and met Zach, who was 15 months old and the first grandchild in his family. During the entire party someone was holding Zach, playing with him, or talking to him. The grandparents played trucks with him, held him on their laps, and read to him. Uncle Charlie chased him around the house, got him cookies, and played trucks with him. Others picked him up to touch the tree, the lights, and gave him toys to play with. That child experienced and felt love constantly that night.

On the way home Anne Marie and I wondered how many children grow up in environments like this. We also talked about how tragic it is that some children never have one day like this.

My motives for bringing this up are not to send anyone back to analyze their childhood, searching for what was right and what was wrong. The point is not to go home, sit down with one's parents, and say, "Mom, Dad, when I was two, how did you treat me? Because if you did not do it right, you messed me up for the rest of my life." No parents do a perfect job, but most do a good enough job.

Our childhoods live on within us. These early experiences are part of what makes us unique and who we are. We get our start with relationships in the family and then the wider circle of relatives, neighbors, and friends. Our childhoods give us strengths and challenges. Some girls grow up tomboys, running all over football fields scoring touchdowns. Some boys prefer to play house or dolls. This does not mean these people are weird or from some other planet.

Some men feel shy around women, others more assertive. Some women feel assertive, comfortable, and confident around men; others don't. Sometimes peers ridicule each other for this and get on each other for being shy or for being aggressive or for not being like everyone else. We need to be careful about criticizing people because they seem different. There is nothing wrong with being shy or with being more aggressive.

MYTH

ANY TEEN WHO ISN'T DATING IS WEIRD.

Some women find it easier to talk to men than women. Some men find it easier to talk to women. Other men and women find it easier to talk with friends of the same sex. Again, there is nothing abnormal about this.

The same is true in regard to dating. Some young people date in their teens; some don't. Teens, often with good intentions, sometimes try to push their friends into dating as if they were trying to cure some disease. My advice to young people feeling pressure to date is this: Don't let people push you into dating if you are not ready. If you have not had 10 dates by sophomore year, you

are not an official, certified loser. There is no national standard to reach. Some teens date earlier, some later. Some date often; others date seldom or never. Teens need to give each other space.

Some, who never or seldom date, have quality friendships with both men and women. These friendships are more valuable than the number of dates.

vithin us.

The quality of relationships is far more important than the number.

In college, I did not date frequently but had many good female friends. We really enjoyed being together. Groups of us males and females went to dances, games, out for pizza. It was a great time and just as valuable as dating.

- With whom among your parent(s), relatives, neighbors, or siblings do you have special bonds?

- Do you find males or females easier to talk to? What topics do you find easier to talk about with members of the same sex? With members of the opposite sex?

- What differences do you experience in the ways males and females talk and listen?

CHAPTER 8

Learning to Touch in America

"We seem to like or even need to be touched, to be reminded that we are alive or that we matter to one another."

—*Richard Rohr,*

"The Holiness of Human Sexuality."

Would you describe your family as no, low, medium, or high touch? Who touches the most in your family? The least? Do males generally touch less or more than females? Why?

Up to the age of five, most of us live in a touch world. People are always grabbing kids, holding them, tickling them, swinging them, or wrestling. These actions don't stop at five, yet around the age of five, we begin to receive messages about when to touch and when not to touch. These can be subtle.

* Richard Rohr, "The Holiness of Human Sexuality," *Sojourners:* October, 1982.

"Devon, you cannot take baths with your sister anymore."

"Why not, Mom?" *"Um...because the bath tub is too small for both of you and the water gets all over the floor."*

Okay, Mom."

School provides messages.

"Jeannie? Please keep your hands to yourself."

"Damon, get your hands off of him."

We need to learn appropriate touch. We can't have 16-year-olds boarding the downtown bus,

roaming up and down the aisles, placing their hands on people's shoulders, arms, or heads as they exclaim, "Hey, how's it going?" Somebody will kill them. We learn when to touch and when not to touch.

Five-year-olds can play and touch at a birthday party in ways older kids can't. At the five-year-olds birthday party seven girls and three boys come. The kids run around, playing a game in the front yard. Somebody slides. Immediately one of the kids jumps on him or her. Soon all the kids are forming one huge hog pile. Parents peer out the front window.

"Oh, look, isn't that cute! The kids are all piling on top of each other. Oh, Peggy just tried to kiss Billy. Hurry, get the camcorder."

All this changes for 18-year-olds. Then, if all the kids pile on top of each other in the front yard, parents will not regard this as cute.

"Oh, my God! What is going on out there? Get off of each other right now! What do you think this is, group sex in the front yard? Get in the house."

Rules about when to touch and when not to touch change. Anyone who goes to live in a foreign land discovers how differently cultures socialize us. For example, suppose because I am a wonderful person, I send all the males in my youth group to southern France for four weeks this summer. I cover the entire cost of the trip. I arrange for them to stay with families in France that have males their age. They will stay close to the French Riviera. I teach them a little French, but I deliberately do not tell them about the culture and customs of southern France.

One of our All-American boys arrives by plane in France. He deplanes with the picture of his French family in his hand. He glances around until he spots them. They have his picture sewn into their retinas. They locate him. As he steps onto the ground, the boy his age runs up to him, puts his arms around him, gives him a big hug, and then kisses him on both cheeks. The American smiles. He politely inquires if there is a phone nearby that he can use. He dials his parents. "Mom, Dad, can you come and get me? I'm stuck living with this weird kid here in France for the next four weeks and need you to come now!" This is normal behavior for men in southern France. Americans are not used to this kind of touch. We shake hands.

I will send the women in my youth group to southern Italy. As the American girls with blonde hair, *le bionde*, are walking around the little village where they will reside with their new Italian sisters, a group of five guys begins to follow them. Soon they begin touching the hair of the Americans, possibly pinching them or grabbing at them. The girls take exception to this.

"Excuse me. Did I say you could touch my hair?"

Their Italian sisters begin swatting the guys and advise the Americans to do the same.

One of the Americans says, "Hit that one, but don't hit that cute one."

AMERICA IS A LOW TOUCH CULTURE.

The Italian women let the American women know that they must stand up for themselves. This may even increase their attractiveness.

Italians touch more than Americans do. Americans visiting Italy often stand out; they are the ones trying to back away from the Italians who are in their faces. Americans prefer talking at a polite distance. The Italians tend to get in one's face to talk. Every culture has its own customs and norms around touch.

America is a low touch culture. The French, the Italians, the Mexicans, most of the people of South America, the Russians, all touch more than we do. Countries such as England and Japan touch less than we do. In Nigeria, the women who work in the fields strap their young babies to them while they work. Many of these children are in direct, daily contact with their mother for the first year or more of their lives.

An article in *Psychology Today* illustrates how touch can vary from culture to culture. The author of the article visited restaurants in various countries. He sat in restaurants for an hour and observed the number of times he saw people touch each other. In Puerto Rico he recorded over 100 instances of touch in one hour. In France he recorded 90. In England none. In America 10.

- **Research the touch patterns of another culture. Interview friends or family members who have come from another country or who have lived in or visited another country.**
  Talk to neighbors or parishioners who are of another culture or who have spent time in another culture.
  Report what you learn.

Our families socialize us in regard to touch. Each family has its own unique patterns of touch. Some families are high touch families, others medium, some low, some none. Some touch positively and some negatively.

I come from a low-touch family. This is not necessarily negative. My parents probably come from low-touch families themselves. By low touch, I mean that I rarely saw my parents kiss on the lips. Sometimes we would see them kiss on the cheek, and we thought, "The hormones are flying today; Mom and Dad kissed on the cheek. It must be their anniversary and we forgot." I never really saw my parents hug or snuggle up together on the couch to watch TV.

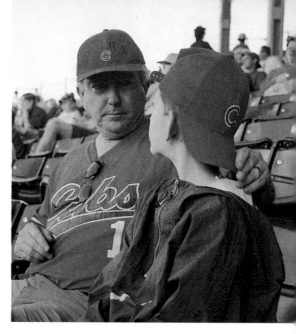

When I first learned about the facts of life, unofficially, in sixth grade, I had trouble buying it. "You're nuts. You are telling me that my parents are doing this in bed? No way. They cannot even touch each other. You come to my house, you live there a week, and you tell me that is happening. There is no way."

I came home and immediately confronted my older sister. "Joan, I just learned about sex, and they said Mom and Dad are doing this..."

She cut me off. "I know, Bobby. When I first learned about sex, I figured it out. We're adopted. Check out the family pictures. How come there are so few pictures of us from zero to nine months?"

I asked to check. "Mom, how come there are no pictures of us from zero to nine months?"

"We didn't have a camera," she answered.

"Yeah, we're adopted," I mumbled under my breath. For the next year we told people we were adopted.

One day my mother came home from grocery shopping. She told my dad that one of the neighbors approached her in the store and told her how special it was that she and her husband would adopt six kids. My mom looked at her neighbor and said, "I wish. The deliveries would have been a lot easier." My mom asked my dad where in the world the neighbor got that idea. My sister and I immediately reminded them of how strange the neighbor was and vacated the room.

When I did some work with physically and emotionally abused kids, I learned first-hand that people will seek out touch in positive or negative ways.

Some people get A's to get touched. Some score touchdowns. Some will be obnoxious to get attention. Others will get sick or in trouble to get noticed. We all need to be loved and touched in some way. It is a fundamental human need. As I observed this, I began to reflect on my own childhood. If my family rarely touched in positive ways, did we touch in negative ways?

I remember sitting on the living room floor, reading the sports page, when my evil, greedy brother would come in and proclaim that he wanted the sports page. I distinctly recall being a saint of a child. I patiently explained to him that I was close to finished and would be happy to bring the paper to him accompanied by orange juice, pancakes, waffles, or whatever breakfast he desired.

"No, I want it now," my evil brother would say.

And I would smile and say, "Come and get it."

He and I would start wrestling. My oldest sister, Joan, frequently came in to break up the fight, but she always got in on it. She joined my brother's side. Then when I was near death, my sister Ellen dove in on my side. My family planned well. We had six kids and could get a tag team going, three-on-three, with team battles on weekends and solo matches during the week. We were constantly wrestling.

There was little hugging or kissing in my family. We kids invented a game called "Stink-Stink." It was not a very original game. One person was the "stink-stink." This person could not run or walk. He or she had to crawl. The other five hid. When the "stink-stink" found one of us, she or he gave the other a hug until the count of three—then that person became a stink-stink, too. The "stink-stinks" multiplied until the last kid to be found had five "stink-stinks" descending upon him or her.

Looking back, I realize although we invented this game for fun, it also took care of touch needs in a healthy way. Our parents never interfered. I also don't think our name for the game was an accident. We called it "stink-stink" because we did not have a real positive image of hugging at that time. When the "stink-stink" grabbed us, it was more like being slimed than hugged.

Families develop patterns of touch. We carry these patterns with us into relationships and life. My wife and I work with engaged couples. Often these couples talk about how one of them is very comfortable with hugging, holding hands, and touching in public, while the other finds it uncomfortable. Encouraging couples to reflect on the touch patterns in their families can provide these couples with insights into their own comfort level with touch. Such reflection can help couples or individuals become aware of the touch patterns they have consciously or unconsciously developed and help them sort out what they wish to hold onto or change, what is helpful and what is not. This process was instructive in my own life.

I was dating the woman I later married. One night, we were leaving a party when she asked me if I was embarrassed to be with her. Being male, I was not able to share that I was falling madly in love with her and contemplating marriage. Instead I said, "No, why do you ask that?" She responded that I never touched her in public.

I could feel fear spread through every limb of my body. I thought to myself, *Touch you in public! Are you nuts? I can't touch you in public!* However, still being male, I managed to calmly respond, "It doesn't seem right. Who wants to walk in on some couple making out on the couch?"

She said, "I'm not asking you to make out with me. I am just asking you to put your arm around me."

I gave her some lame excuse that she bought for about three days. However, I could not shake her question. Why did fear engulf my entire being when she mentioned touching in public? I had to do my homework to uncover the source. I did not know how to touch. It had never really been modeled to me. I reflected on my own learned patterns of touch. I wanted to be able to touch more naturally in public. This was a pattern I chose to work on and change. Though I was able to change it, I doubt my fear will ever totally disappear.

- What appeals to you or repels you about joining in mosh pits at rock concerts? How do you feel about body surfing and the push of circling crowd movement? Should both boys and girls participate?

- Observe in the school cafeteria, in the halls, at sports events, how much and what kind of touching occurs. Do females touch more often or males? Do females and males touch differently? The same?

- What kind of touch is comfortable among friends? What kind do you not like?

- Do adults touch students? If yes, how? Do students touch adults? If so, how?

- Do students touch students more than adults touch adults?

- Overall, do you think there is more touch among your peer group than among adults? If so, why? What changes?

We need to understand and appreciate the role touch plays in our lives. Touch can heal. If I were a high school principal, I would hire a professional masseuse to teach students how massage can soothe headaches or relieve tension without the use of medications. This person could teach the benefits of a good hand massage, foot massage, or back rub.

New York City Hospitals experimented with hiring professional masseuses to help deal with patients who complained of chronic neck, back, and shoulder pain. One group of patients were treated with regular prescription medications. The other half were given professional massages. Those who were treated with massage returned to the hospital less frequently, and complained of pain less often than those on the medications.

TOUCH HAS THE POWER TO HURT OR HEAL.

As a volunteer at a nursing home, I experienced the value of touch for a woman suffering from senility. I was assigned to three patients, one of whom was Rose. When I came to visit her, she often called me Emily, the name of her daughter. She never looked me in the eye. Instead she looked off at the wall or ceiling while she spoke to me. She sometimes got excited, chattering wildly, frantically waving her hands in the air. I had no clue what she was carrying on about.

The nursing home asked volunteers to spend at least 15 minutes a visit with each person. I spent less and less time with Rose, reducing my visits to 5 minutes or less. I felt that it was a waste of time. The other two people I visited at least knew who I was.

At one of my obligatory, abbreviated visits, Rose as usual greeted me as Emily, stared right past me at the wall, and flailed her hands meaninglessly in the air. In exasperation, I took hold of her hands, held them on my knees, and told her I was not her daughter. My name was Bob. As I held her hands in mine, she calmed down. For the first time she looked right into my eyes.

There were no miracles. She continued to call me Emily, yet I discovered that when I held her hands she could talk to me. She looked into my eyes. The visits grew more pleasant. She told me stories of her life, of how she grew up in a time very different from mine. The 15 minutes went by quickly. Touch helped Rose focus and connect with me.

Cases of sexual abuse and sexual harassment have made people today rightly very wary about touch. Fearful of law suits, some school districts no longer allow teachers to touch students in any way. Professions are establishing guidelines for employees regarding touch in the work place. Working with victims of abuse reminds me not to minimize how important it is for people to stand up for themselves when they feel they are being harassed.

However, healthy touch has the power to heal, comfort, relax, and empower. Touch has too many benefits to be completely eliminated or so stringently regulated that it loses all spontaneity. Touch should never be forced on another, but it may be equally destructive to force it out of all our human interactions.

In the 1960s, Sydney Simon coined a phrase "skin hunger." This phrase referred to people who would go years without touching or being touched. Claudia Schmidt, a musician, wrote a song entitled "Skin Gangsters" that gives life to Simon's phrase.

HEALTHY TOUCH HAS THE POWER TO HEAL, COMFORT, RELAX, AND EMPOWER.

In this song, Schmidt tells of being abandoned by her parents. She grew up in an all female orphanage in which the girls experienced little human contact. She sings about how she and the other girls become "skin gangsters," plotting ways to steal human touch. She describes groups of girls walking down the hall and spotting an adult coming toward them. They waited and pushed one of their group into the person walking by to steal touch. During the night, some of the five, six, and seven year olds waited until the lights were turned off and the moderators asleep, then stole into each other's beds to have a warm body to curl up next to.

One of the people Claudia Schmidt fondly recalls from the orphanage was a woman who gave out food in the cafeteria. She was a large African-American woman who singled out every third or fourth girl as she came through the line for her food and said to her that she looked like she could use a hug today. Schmidt describes the hugs of this woman as "being enveloped in this flesh," a memory she has never forgotten.

We humans have a basic need for touch. We need to develop and encourage healthy ways to touch each other. As our world becomes increasingly high tech, the need for high touch also grows. As we increase our use of computers and machines at work, we need to compensate with aerobics, lunchtime volleyball, and other high-touch opportunities for employees to keep their sanity, to stay in touch with other humans.

- In the past, people, especially women, have been harassed in the workplace. Many of these people felt trapped because, if they complained, they risked losing their jobs. Today, people are more aware of sexual harassment. In your mind, what constitutes sexual harassment?

- What are the benefits of present sexual-harassment policies in high school? What are some of the problems?

- What examples can you give of healthy touch having a positive effect on you?

CHAPTER 9

Intimacy

Begin this section by brainstorming what the word *intimacy* means to members of your group. Brainstorming rules allow any and all answers and forbid any criticism. List on a chalkboard or piece of paper all the meanings group members can come up with.

"Sexuality is the Creator's ingenious way of calling us constantly out of ourselves into relationship with one another."
—Human Sexuality, New Directions, in American Catholic Thought*

The preceding chapters build a case for how naturally we human beings seek touch, affection, and love. As young people move into the senior-high years and beyond, I believe that intimacy is what they are looking for in relationships. We want to find others with whom we can connect, be ourselves, and have fun.

* Human Sexuality, New Directions in American Catholic Thought: A Study Commissioned by the Catholic Theological Society of America, Anthony Kosnik, Chair. NY: Paulist Press, 1977.

The word *intimacy* derives from the Latin word *timeo*, which mean *fear*. The *in* is a negative as in the word *intolerance*. Thus the word *in-timacy* literally means *no fear, without fear*. Anyone who has ever truly been in love knows intimacy is scary. No one can hurt us more than someone we are close to.

■ **How true is it in your experience that the people you are closest to can hurt you? If so, how can they hurt you? If not, why not? Has someone you were not close to hurt you?**

I leave my job at the end of the day. I go out to my car, and a van pulls up. On the side of the van is an inscription which reads: The Really Poor Self-Esteem Club. Five people, whom I have never met before, pile out of the van. The apparent leader comes toward me and points to me.

"Now, all of you in this group who feel crummy about yourselves, look at this guy. Don't you feel better about yourselves now? You could be him. Any time you are feeling bad about yourself, just think, at least I am not as bad off as he is. Have you ever seen anyone so pathetic?"

Then, as they all pile back into the van, I say, "Just because I am a sex symbol, you don't need to be intimidated."
They drive off.

Seriously, if this happened, I would not be thrilled, but it would not bother me that much. However, if these people were my close friends, my wife, my kids, or my birth family, and they sincerely meant it, it would hurt big time.

MYTH

SEX AND INTIMACY ARE THE SAME THING.

People we are intimate with can hurt us more than anyone else. The number one trigger for suicide among high-school males is the breakup with a girlfriend. Breaking up with a boyfriend or girlfriend can be a crushing experience.

Our culture incorrectly equates the word *intimacy* with *sex*. The frequent legal term for sexual intercourse is intimacy. I was summoned into court to testify on behalf of a client. Attempting to call into question the character of one of the witnesses, the attorney asked, "Mrs. Johnson, on December 14th, were you not intimate with a man other than your husband?" The attorney was asking if she had sex with someone else.

Sex and intimacy are not necessarily synonymous. People can have sex and never be intimate. People can be intimate and never have sex.

■ **Ask two people over the age of 21 their definition of intimacy. Share your definitions with your class. Pick out definitions you really agree or disagree with.**

I believe most adults and teens today are not looking for sex. This may sound incredibly naive in today's culture. When I make this statement in class, I can always count on a few students staring at me as if they had just watched some alien suck out my brain. However, based on my experience of working with adolescents and adults, I believe people are not looking for sex as much as they are searching for intimacy.

Many people settle for sex because they don't believe that intimacy is possible. They settle for sex because they don't believe they are worth any more than that. They settle for sex because intimacy is too difficult or too frightening. They settle for sex because it is easier, less complicated, and more concrete. They settle for sex for any number of reasons, yet what they really want and need is intimacy.

A married couple came to see me for counseling. The marriage was into its second year. Both were attractive people. They admitted they were having

70

trouble with sex. They found explaining the problem embarrassing. Finally, the woman broke the ice. She explained that when they first married, sex was great. She began to sense a change after about a year. She said sex was fine when he initiated, but when she initiated, he seemed increasingly distant and agitated. At first, he went along, but she sensed that he was going through the motions for her. Eventually it worsened to the point that she felt when she flirted with him or was affectionate toward him, he was uncomfortable to the point of repulsion. She felt as if he were no longer interested in her.

MANY PEOPLE SETTLE FOR SEX BECAUSE THEY DON'T BELIEVE THAT INTIMACY IS POSSIBLE.

I asked him about this. I joked that if this attractive woman wanted me, I would be honored. He acknowledged that her advances turned him off, but he didn't know why. She said this was the same response he gave her. I asked if he was traditional. Woman runs, man pursues. He said no. I was stuck. So I did what all counselors are supposed to do when they are stymied. I went into family backgrounds.

She had grown up in an alcoholic family. She had recently started in a program called "Adult Children of Alcoholics." I stopped her at this point, because I was sure I was onto something. I asked her how long she had been in the program, and she speculated about six months. I turned to him and asked if he had noticed any changes in her since she started the program.

"Changes!" he exclaimed. "God, did she change. She used to be like a little girl to me. She had me on this pedestal. She seemed to worship every-thing about me. Now if she is angry, she tells me. If she is hurt, she tells me. If she is happy, she tells me. You want to know what she is thinking, just ask, she'll tell you." I looked right at him and said, "And you don't like the change."

"No," he said, "I like it."

This threw me. I thought I had this great insight for them. I was tempted to call him a liar and tell him he was into denial, but I didn't know either of them well enough to do it.

"You like the change?" I repeated, groping for a confession, but his answer did not change. Then I inquired about his family history and learned that he had been an addict himself. He started with alcohol his sophomore year of high school. He progressed into acid and cocaine, until going straight his sophomore year of college. He had been straight for seven years and was still in an AA group. I turned to her and asked

if she knew when he was happy, hurt, sad.

"No," she said thoughtfully. "I never know what he is feeling. He doesn't share his feelings."

We talked more about this. I suggested that maybe the sexual problem was connected to his not letting her in emotionally. I thought their physical problems might be manifesting this emotional distance. He was not letting her in, letting her get close. He was shutting her out emotionally and physically. Perhaps he felt that she did not just want his body; she wanted his soul.

He looked at me as if I had spoken a foreign language. "She wants my soul?"

"Yes," I answered. "I mean, she can't go into your body, remove your soul, and hang it next to her fireplace like some kind of trophy fish. Intimacy is not just about rubbing bodies together; it is also rubbing souls. She wants to rub souls with you. She wants to know who you really are in there, what you're feeling, thinking, what's going on in there. It gets cold where she is. She wants in."

SEXUAL PROBLEMS USUALLY INDICATE INTIMACY PROBLEMS.

She nodded. "That's it. That's it."

He stared at both of us as if we were in some conspiracy against him. "She wants my soul?" he repeated.

We nodded. For about 30 minutes both of us tried to explain it to him. Finally, he held up his hands in mock surrender.

"She wants my soul," he recited knowingly.

"Yes," she said.

"I'm sorry," he said, looking right into her. "Nobody gets that close."

"Then I can't be married to you," she replied, with obvious pain.

"Time out," I interjected. "This is new stuff for both of you. Can you give him time to work on this? Can you understand where she is coming from? Can you give yourselves time?" They both agreed to take some time to work on this. They are still working.

This couple was not looking for sex. They had sex, all the sex they wanted. The woman was looking for something deeper. The sex wasn't the problem. But sex served as a barometer of the relationship, as it often can. The physical distance he wanted was a symptom of wanting emotional distance. Sexual problems, unless they are physical, usually indicate an intimacy problem.

The week contains 168 hours. According to a recent study reported in the book, *Supermarital Sex*, (an awful title but not a bad book), the average couple in America, whether married or living together engages in sexual intercourse an average of 2 to 3 hours a week. This includes activity leading to sexual intercourse. My students greeted these statistics with disbelief. Let us say my students who want to dedicate themselves to changing these statistics succeed in doubling the national average to 4 or 6 hours a week. That still leaves the normal couple in America with 162 hours. Sleep accounts for 56 of those hours, work another 40 or more. If all couples have going for them is sex, life can get pretty boring during the remaining 66 hours.

> SEX IS AN ACT; SEXUALITY IS WHO WE ARE.

Sex is just one small part of our sexuality. Our sexuality is the way we talk, breathe, walk, play, how we interact with others, how we laugh, and how we cry. Sex is an act; sexuality is who we are.

When we begin to understand that our sexuality has to do with our whole being and not just sex, it is easier to see how the Jesus of the gospels modeled healthy intimacy. Jesus engaged people, reached out to a diversity of people, and had close friends. He wept when Lazarus died. He interacted with the woman at the well. He forgave Peter when he betrayed him. Jesus was constantly intimate with people, but his intimacy did not involve sex. Intimacy is not tied to sex. The story of the woman caught in adultery brings out this point. In fact, it is interesting that the man with whom she was sexual is nowhere to be found. The man Jesus, with whom she is not sexual, is very much there for her.

Accusers drag the woman before Jesus to be stoned. Jesus writes in the dirt and invites anyone who has not sinned to begin the stoning. All walk away. Jesus is left with this woman standing before him, stripped of her dignity. Jesus asks who condemns her. She answers that no one has. Jesus tells her he will not condemn her either and instructs her to avoid this sin in the future.

This story is rich in emotional intimacy. Jesus senses her shame and humiliation. She sees her deepest self. She recognizes her desire to live differently. Their meeting is a deep, life-changing, intimate encounter.

The story is one of numerous scenes in which Jesus is intimate with another person. Jesus recognizes that his friend Peter, who speaks openly of his loyalty, will deny their friendship. Jesus' conversation with the Samaritan woman at the well leads her to recognize who he is and believe in him. Jesus accepts the deep sorrow of the sinful woman who washes his feet with her tears. Jesus was intimate with a great number of both men and women.

■ Find and read one of the stories mentioned above in the gospels: the woman taken in adultery, John 8.1-11; Peter's denial, Mark 14.27-31, 66-72; the Samaritan woman, John 4.1-42; the sinful woman, Luke 7.36-50. Identify examples of intimacy in the story you choose to read.

CHAPTER 10

Unhealthy Patterns of Intimacy

Keep a personal and private log like the one below for a week. List the people you spend time with each day. Write in the first column the names of those you see alone. Write in the second column those you see in groups. Evaluate the patterns you see at the end of the week. Are you seeing the friends you value most? Are you spending too much time with one person and not enough with others?

Day	Alone	Group
Monday		
Tuesday		
Wednesday		
Thursday		
Friday		
Saturday		
Sunday		

"Unfortunately, it seems that what you deny and repress is in fact what controls and forms you. We have refused to dialogue, listen to, accept, and relate to our sexuality positively. Now we find ourselves awkward and out of touch with its positive meaning. It haunts us from its shadowed position."

—*Richard Rohr,* "The Holiness of Human Sexuality. "*

Intimacy has many dimensions. We experience intimacy with family members. This intimacy differs from intimacy with friends. Friends who grow up together often have memories, traditions, common interests that make their closeness different from bonds between friends made in high school. Intimacy can form within a youth group or a sports team. Kinds of intimacy evolve from working on a play together or singing in a choir. Junior high and high school students are establishing patterns of intimacy that they will carry into present and future relationships.

A teacher colleague, Mike Shimek, divides intimacy into two categories—genital patterns of intimacy and integrated patterns of intimacy. Genital patterns refer to unhealthy patterns; integrated, to healthy patterns.

Genital patterns of intimacy are not always unhealthy. When they appear within the context of integrated intimacy, they can be life giving. When people separate genital intimacy from the rest of their lives, the pattern can be harmful.

* Richard Rohr, "The Holiness of Human Sexuality," *Sojourners*. October, 1982.

In unhealthy patterns of intimacy, a young person focuses his or her personality, charm, good looks, and energies on getting another person to have genital sex. The unhealthy patterns are those we turn on when we want something—the manipulation games.

Here's an exaggerated example. You go home to your parent or parents. You ask to sit down and talk. "Mom, Dad, I feel bad that I neglected to thank you for working 40 hours last week for our family. I admire how every morning you get up, go to work, and bring home the money to share with us. And the house looks great. How do you do it? Go to work, keep the house up, you are truly amazing. And the menu selection this week was superb. I really enjoyed the meals."

Your parents respond, "What do you want?"

You feign slight offense, then get to the heart of the matter. "All the kids are going to this guy's beach house this weekend. All the kids from church are going, and everybody's parents have said yes but you. There are going to be 10 chaperones per kid, we are to bring our Bibles along, and I wondered if I could go?" You flutter your eyes and conjure up the sweetest smile.

When my students want an extension for an assignment, they often turn on the excuses.

"Mr. Bartlett? The assignment that was due today? I was just sitting down to do it last night when my church called and asked if I could help feed the homeless at the shelter. I had just finished at the shelter and was rushing home to do my assignment when the pastor of my church stopped me and asked me if I could help him prepare his homily for Sunday. After that I headed right home when all at once a four-car accident happened right in front of me. I rushed over and pulled 11 bodies out of the burning wrecks seconds before their cars exploded, gave them CPR, carried them to the hospital, and never finished my assignment. Could I hand it in tomorrow?"

I let them know that I would be honored if they gave me their assignment sometime before they graduate. This way I will at least have a relic of this saint who graced my classroom.

All of us can turn it on when we want something. Sometimes there is no harm in this. It can be fun and humorous to flirt with or be sugary sweet to someone to get him or her to help us, especially if we know we are doing it and so does the other person. For example, I return a movie video late and try to get the check-in person not to charge me a late fee. We all do it.

Imagine how you'd react on a date like the following.

She sits in front of a mirror attempting to reach perfection with her hair, when she hears his car pull up. The car horn blares. Usually he comes to the door, but tonight he is running late. Dad only begins his lecture about the guy not coming to the door before she brushes quickly past him and bounds out to the car.

As she gets in the car, she quickly senses her date is not in a great mood. He does manage to mumble "hi" and tells her she looks nice. His words lack sincerity. She says "hi" back and lets him know she is glad to see him. They pull out of the driveway. On the way to dinner and a movie, he tells her he has to stop at a party and talk to a friend. "No problem," she says.

They park at the house of the party. He does not open the door for her, but hey, who does anymore? He begins walking into the house without waiting for her. She rushes to catch up to him just in time to have the screen

door bang in her face. She enters the house, surveys the faces assembled, but does not see one face that she recognizes. Then she spots her date sitting in the middle of a card game next to a guy who looks familiar.

Before long, he is participating in the card game. She stands behind him, feeling like some Las Vegas show girl, but he doesn't seem to notice. She gently rubs his shoulder as she asks how long before they leave. He assures her they will leave in minutes.

The minutes feel like hours. She mentions to him that she feels uncomfortable. He apologizes and then introduces her to the table as his girlfriend without mentioning her name. She smiles like a beauty queen on a float.

After what seems an eternity, she drops a hint to him that she is getting hungry. He directs her to help herself to the food in the refrigerator and asks her to bring him something to drink. She is now becoming the waitress. She is angry and lets him know that she is leaving with or without him, preferably the latter. He tells the boys at the table that this is his last hand, that he has to get going.

As they walk out to the car, he once again does not walk with her but in front of her. Instead of driving to the agreed-upon restaurant, he pulls the car over and for the first time he really looks at her. He tells her how great she looks and leans over to kiss her. If she has any sense of self-respect, she puts both her hands up and informs him that if he comes any nearer, he will never walk or breathe again.

"All night you treat me like I don't exist, and now when you want something, you turn it on. Just take me home."

This fellow demonstrated genital patterns. He turns on compliments and attention when he wants sex.

Here's an example from real life.

> I had a roommate in college who demonstrated genital patterns. He went out one night to a bar, came home about 12:30 A.M., and burst into our room.
>
> "You guys, I just met the most beautiful woman in the world!"
>
> In the room were six of us losers. We had remained in our dorm room studying on Friday night, not because we wanted to be geniuses, but because we had nothing better to do. Our big highlight was to go to White Castle and get some "sliders" (also known as burgers). I glanced up at my roommate and asked what her name was.
>
> "Joan. Her name is Joan. And I don't believe in love at first sight, but it just happened! We could talk about anything. It was like we had known each other our entire lives. Sense of humor; I had her laughing; she had me laughing. And we have things in common. She has her own downhill ski equipment; we are talking cheap date here, and we are going to the basketball game next Saturday."
>
> We were jealous, but it was exciting to see him so pumped. We were happy for him that he had met someone. We started praying that we would have a similar experience prior to turning 80.
>
> Next Saturday came and the losers began to congregate in my room. My roommate was grooming intensely for his date. Have you ever noticed how winners always ask those deeply sensitive questions of losers? My roommate was primping in front of his mirror.
>
> "Hey, what are you guys doing tonight?" he asked.
>
> The other losers and I glared at him.
>
> "Us? Why, there are 621 women coming from the university to attack us, and then we're going to White Castle." He smiled and left.
>
> He returned about 10:30 P.M., threw open the door, and surveyed us as if

we were some new strain of pond scum or something. He grabbed his TV and turned it on full blast. He turned his stereo on full blast, too, then fell on his bed with his arms folded, staring at the ceiling. He pulled out a paper bag, extracted a six-pack of beer, and began downing one beer after another.

I didn't have to be in counseling or the perceptive person that I am to pick up tension in the room, big time.

"Mike. You're home early," I said, trying to break the silence.

"You're observant," he snorted back. It is hard not to be when you live in a closet together in college.

"Where's Joan?" I asked.

"I don't know, and I don't care," he growled back. "The most beautiful woman in the world."

"Did you have a fight?"

"Yeah, you're really perceptive," he shot back.

"What was the fight about?" I asked.

"She doesn't love me anymore, okay?" he said, shaking his head disgustedly at me as if I were the only human who had not yet come to this realization.

"She said that to you? She said she didn't love you?" I said in disbelief.

"No, stupid, I could tell," he answered sarcastically.

Us losers don't often get into these situations. "How could you tell?"

"I could tell," he said with irritation.

"How?" I insisted.

"I tried to feel her up and she wouldn't let me, okay?" he said, shaking his head in utter disdain.

"If a girl is not comfortable with petting on the second date, she doesn't love you?" I wanted to be sarcastic and explain, "Hey, you know what is wrong with this woman? She must have self-respect, values. She believes in getting to know someone, in developing a friendship first. She respects herself enough not to let guys use her."

I felt like grabbing my roommate, holding him up against the wall, and gently slapping each side of his face a dozen times, in the way one tries to sober up a drunk. I wanted to say, 'Mike, you are into genital patterns. You left for this date with one thing on your mind, "I'm going to feel her up. It's my way or the highway, honey, or it is not a successful date.'" I wanted to say, "Why don't you take Joan's head off, place it on a shelf, take her breasts, and feel her up. It's not like you want to deal with a real human being, a whole person."

But to be honest, I felt sorry to him. Here he had a woman with whom he could sit and talk about anything, could laugh, and shared common interests. He threw this all out the window. I wanted to scream into his face, *You're an idiot. For all you have taken the trouble to know about her, maybe she just learned that morning that her mother was terminally ill.*

"Oh, your mother is sick? I'm sorry. You want to go make out?"

"Sure," she is supposed to respond. "I always find people to make out with when someone in my family is sick."

Patterns of intimacy are unhealthy when a man or woman loves someone for what that person will do for him or her, not for who the person is. I learned this well working with pregnant girls.

I asked one girl what happened.

"I think you can figure out what happened," came the exasperated reply.

"Yes, I can figure that part out. I mean how did you get to the point of having sex?" I asked.

Am I being loved

"I was going out with this guy, and he was different from any guy I ever met. We had fun. We weren't just going to movies and stuff; we were going to dances and concerts. I could tell him anything, and he could tell me. He knew me better than my own family, and I knew him."

"This sounds great. What happened?" I asked.

"After about two months, he said that if we really loved each other, we needed to show it more. I loved him, so we did. We went further. But that wasn't enough. We started having sex, and I got pregnant."

"Where is this guy who loves you?" I inquired.

"He's scared. He doesn't know what to do. He doesn't want people to know that he is the father until I decide what I am going to do."

"Is he going to support you?" I interrupted.

"He said if I get an abortion, he would pay for it."

"Is that what you want to do?" I asked.

"I don't know. Do you think he used me?"

This question comes up often. I don't like adding to a hurting person's pain.

"I don't think he used you at first. It seems as if you had a pretty good relationship. But when the 'If you love me, you'll do this' started, I think you got used."

The words "if you love me" signal danger. When someone says, "If you love me, you should show it more or do this," red flags should go up. This is the signal to ask yourself: Am I being loved for who I am or what I will do? It is also the signal to ask the other person, "You mean if I say no, you're walking away? It has to be your way or nothing? What kind of relationship is this?"

If I am in a healthy relationship, I can say yes or no and the other person respects my wishes. No one who cares about me will push me or try to talk me into things I do not want to do.

or who I am?

Conversations with these pregnant girls revealed that they did not have sex because they thought this was going to be the greatest thing in the world. They had sex to keep a close intimate relationship going. Many felt that if they gave the guy what he wanted, they could keep him around.

Typically, the young women found it nice to have someone who called them, who talked to them, who told them they were pretty, who wanted to spend time with them. They desired the intimacy and tried to get it through the sex. But this is backwards.

Intimacy needs to come before sex. In healthy relationships the emphasis is on developing a friendship and having fun doing things together and with others.

Sex is a celebration of an intimate, committed relationship. That's my definition of a marriage—the faithful, mutual giving of two persons to each other and to children they welcome and take responsibility to raise and love. Without intimacy and commitment in a relationship, sex loses the power to connect and to build. It gets reduced to the using of another person for personal pleasure.

Many popular films put sex before intimacy. Characters have sex within the first 10 minutes of meeting each other and then gradually get to know each other. I want to stand up at these films and yell at them to rewind to the first sex scene. I want to ask the characters in the film what the sex was like before they knew each other and what it was like after they really got to know each other. I believe almost all would prefer the sex that came after the characters established a deep relationship.

The media, at times, can feed into the myth that sex is love and love is sex. The media did not create this myth; it has existed as long as us humans, but the media can contribute to it.

That sex is love is simply not true. Without commitment, sex is a false attempt to reach out from ourselves. Sex can become solely for one person's pleasure with no regard for the partner. There is no rubbing of souls. Sex without intimacy is not as passionate or as fulfilling, and it loses its sacredness. Substituting sex for intimacy is all too common. It is sad to witness young people doing this without even realizing it. This pattern can cross over into adult relationships. We place far too much emphasis on sex instead of intimacy.

MYTH

SEX IS LOVE;
LOVE IS SEX.

Intimacy needs to come before sex. Closeness, friendship, and the baring of souls need to take place before the sex, and then the sex can celebrate what is already there.

No one has ever died from a lack of sex, although people may feel as if they will from time to time, but people have died from a lack of intimacy. This is why the Church expects couples to commit to each other in marriage before they get sexually involved.

■ **How can sex get in the way of or be used to avoid intimacy? Give examples.**

Sex can actually be used to avoid real intimacy. I worked with a young woman who described this reality.

She had been sexually abused by her gymnastics coach at the age of 13. He did not have sexual intercourse with her but had fondled her. She never told anyone. A few years later, she started a relationship with a guy she met. She felt guilty because she had done more with this coach, whom she never loved, than she had with this guy for whom she felt love.

The two met at a football game and began going to the games together. They had fun at the games, watching and socializing with people in their class. It became their ritual to go to the games and join their friends for pizza after the game.

One Friday night, he picked her up at her house to go to the game. She discovered she had forgotten something. They went back to her house to get it.

Meanwhile, her parents had decided to go out themselves because none of the kids were home and they were free. She and her date returned to an empty house. She had her key, found what she needed, and without planning, they began kissing and were late for the

game. This kicked off what was to become a weekly ritual of sex.

When she later came to me for counseling, she could look back and see that having sex was the beginning of the end for them. She said sex became the focus of their relationship. They stopped attending the games, did not go out with the friends, and stopped having fun. She said that within a couple of weeks all they centered on was sex. It was easier for them to have sex than to talk to each other, to share feelings, to plan dates.

In counseling, this young woman remarked that she could not even tell him that she was not comfortable with what they were doing. She discovered after they broke up that neither was he. The sex was not even pleasurable anymore. She described enduring sex, him getting excited and her mentally somewhere else, just going through the motions. The gap between them widened until they broke up.

Reflecting back on this experience, she felt the sex hurt their relationship. It was easy and inexpensive. It was easier to have sex than to talk or share feelings. It grew into a rut that both disliked but neither could express. Sex can get in the way of real intimacy.

Most of my examples have focused on men using women. Woman can also use men.

I had a high school student who was upset come to see me. His former girlfriend had wanted to have sex with him. He did not feel he was ready. She grew angry at his refusal and threatened to spread rumors around the school that he was not man enough to do it, that he was gay. He still refused, and she launched the rumors. He felt helpless to stop them. Eventually the rumors died naturally, yet he was still grieving the loss of her and what they had.

I also met with a man in his 20s who was experiencing a dating drought. He was beginning to wonder if he would ever date again. At a party an attractive woman began talking to him. He felt they were hitting it off but did not want to set himself up for disappointment.

The more they talked, the more energy he felt between them. They danced together, continued to talk, and she asked him to bring her home. She invited him in for coffee and initiated sex with him. He could not believe it. They saw each other every night for the next two weeks. He brought her to meet his parents and began to look for an engagement ring.

She called him to cancel a Friday night date. He was upset. She explained that she had to go to California. She'd had a fight with her roommate and her roommate had taken off for California. She had to go to get some of her stuff the roommate had taken and also hoped to patch things up. He offered to go with her, but she felt she had to do this on her own.

> GETTING USED HURTS, WHETHER YOU ARE MALE OR FEMALE.

He found out later that everything was true, except that the roommate was her fiancé. They had been going out for two years and were to be married in two months when he got mad and broke the engagement off. He left her a note referring to her as a female animal and left for California.

The night her fiancé left was the night she met this guy at the party. Instead of talking to her friends about what happened, rather than grieving over her loss of intimacy, she filled her emptiness by getting into a relationship with this new guy.

She left for California where she and her fiancé successfully reconciled. They rescheduled the wedding, and in a "sensitive" move sent the man she met at the party a wedding invitation. The invitation devastated him. He then began to piece together how she used him to fill the intimacy hole in her life. She substituted sex for the intimacy she had lost.

Once when I was telling this story to a high school class, I overheard one male say, "Use me, use me." Having sex may sound fun, but getting used hurts, whether you are male or female. When I give myself to someone and that person abuses my gift, it hurts. If getting used doesn't hurt, then I never really did give myself to the other person.

Reflecting on our patterns of intimacy can help us identify patterns or behaviors we don't want. If we center on ourselves, our sexuality will focus on our needs, our desires, our agendas without regard for the needs, wants, and desires of those we are in relationship with. If we are shallow and superficial, we will lack the ability and desire to get to know others and deepen relationships. We will manipulate, use, and discard supposed friends. If we do not know how to have close meaningful friendships, this will show up in our sexuality. We won't know how to hang in there and sustain relationships during hard times. If we have the courage to examine our patterns honestly, our insights can help us learn to be more intimate in healthy ways.

We also have to reflect on the patterns of intimacy of the people we are in relationships with. If their patterns are unhealthy, we need to point this out, so they can learn and grow. If they refuse to listen, the relationship needs time out for working on the problem. If they refuse to work on sharing more deeply or taking more interest, the relationship is not that important to them. We then need to call a temporary or even permanent halt to the relationship.

- Who uses the other more, men or women?

- Do women use men in a different way than men use women?

- Have you ever observed people using other people? What stops you from doing this also? Do you think these people who use others will have long-term consequences to deal with? What might some of these be?

CHAPTER 11

Using People Hurts

Before reading and discussing this chapter, identify three things you definitely do not want in your relationships.

"We will learn how to be properly sexual as we understand the properly passionate relationship that God has with us. And we will learn how to be properly spiritual as we come to understand the true character of human longing and affection . . . God's passion created ours . . . If we are afraid of our sexuality, we are afraid of God."

—*Father Richard Rohr,* Near Occasion of Grace. *

Most of us hear some wonderful lines in our lives. "Hey, I'm 18; you're 18. We're adults. We have biological needs. How about a little one-on-one tonight? Just you and me. I don't love you. You don't love me. We're up front. We're honest. No one gets hurt. You're nervous? No problem. Just relax. What do

---

*Father Richard Rohr, *Near Occasion of Grace.* Maryknoll, NY: Orbis Books, 1998.

you like? Beer? Wine coolers? I'll supply. We'll just have a little fun.
No one gets hurt."

When I was in college, I thought this line might be true. I tended to
assume that if both people were up front and honest, no one would be hurt.
As a counselor, I have come to believe this is rarely true. Usually one person
gets hurt, if not both.

Play out the assumption, "We have biological needs..." How romantic a
thought is that? How special is being compared to eating an omelet or going to
the bathroom—other biological needs? How many of us have as a goal in our
lives to become someone's biological-need provider? Imagine the
wedding vows, "I promise to be your biological-need provider
forever and ever."

**GETTING
USED
STINKS!**

If you use lines that promise no one will get hurt or someone
uses them on you and the proposal works, think twice. Take
your faith seriously that teaches against premarital sex. Using
someone is a wrong relationship, what the Christian community calls a sin.
Such behavior is self-centered, self-serving. The relationship centers on what I
want and what I can get, not on who the other person is.

Take your own experience seriously, too. Having someone use us for our
clothes, our car, our money, or our brains upsets most of us. If someone treats
us well simply to get rides or to become friends with one of our friends, we feel
angry. Getting used stinks.

Hopefully, people who get upset about being used for their cars or friends
will feel just as upset about someone using them for their bodies. We are each
created in the image and likeness of God; no one has the right to use us, nor do
we have the right to use someone else.

Often the people who do not get upset about being used have self-esteem
about the size of a dime. The last thing they need is for someone to use them
and then discard them. Such treatment will further damage their self-image.

A person who is using sex to gain love and acceptance is not going to get what he or she wants or needs. Unfortunately, using relationships only deepen the hole of loneliness and alienation.

People who knowingly take advantage of others and use them for their own pleasure may be perilously close to those to whom Jesus said, "It would be better to have a great millstone hung around your neck and be thrown into the sea than to lead one of my little ones astray" (Matthew 18.6).

Students have labels in schools. The words used change, but the meanings do not.

"She'll do it with anybody. She's really loose, a 'ho. If you're looking for a good time on a Friday night, just give her a call."

"That guy is a real stud, a real player. He has knocked up over half the girls in the school and now is going after all the women in the conference."

In my counseling work, I have discovered that many young people who get labeled this way are dealing with some serious circumstances. Many have been physically or sexually abused, some as early as age three or four. They have grown up in unhealthy patterns of being used and victimized. For some, being used is all they know. It becomes an unconscious pattern. They don't deserve the labels others give them any more than they deserved the abuse.

I am not asking you to take on young people in trouble as your best friends. I am not asking you to adopt them as your Confirmation service project, but at least don't label them or use them. It is not what they need.

When someone says she is a 'ho or he is a stud, ask why. I wonder why they are doing that. I wonder what they are looking for or what they live with. At least stretch yourself and others to look deeper into this person. There usually is much more there.

I once had a high school student come into my office when I was working in a parish. He had attended some of our youth activities. He placed a sheet of paper with the names of 13 girls on my desk.

I said, "What's this?"

He said, "I just saw the doctor, and he told me I have a sexually transmitted disease. Anyone I have had sex with in the last couple of months could have it. I had sex with these 13 girls in the last few months."

He caught me off guard. "Well, congratulations. What did you want me to do? Put these names in the parish bulletin?"

He stared right into me. "No. The doctor said that these girls could have the disease and not know it. The doctor said they should be notified. These girls could be sick and not know it. You say you care about kids, so I thought you might want to notify them."

"You want me to notify them? What, I have sucker written all over my forehead?" I asked. "I have a great idea. I have a phone over here in the corner which you can use for free. You have the phone numbers of all these women written right after their names. I'll tell you what. You can use my phone and call them. I will support you and cheer you on. I'm sure they will be glad to hear from you."

CASUAL SEX IS A USING RELATIONSHIP.

He shook his head. "Listen. If you care about these girls, you will call them. They could be sick and not know it. You're their last chance, because if you don't call them, they don't get called. When I leave here, I am ripping up this list."

I was young. I also believe that God walks with me or I would not go near the messes I get into. The next thing out of my mouth was, "I'll call them. If you come and see me three times." He consented.

The next three sessions were not among my most memorable. He let me know what a loser I was—in slightly more colorful language. In the third session, I said something that hurt him. I knew immediately, because his body tightened up. He was no longer sneering at me, and I sensed he was fighting back tears. Mentally, I was scrambling. I was feverishly reviewing what I previously had said in order to pinpoint what had hurt him. I wanted to focus in

on it and break open what this pain was about.

I thought I had it and hit him with it. I missed. Instead of breaking him, he got mad, "Who the hell do you think you are? You some kind of sex expert or something? How many women have you gone all the way with?"

Oh, God, I thought to myself. He is going to real impressed with my answer- 5,284 in 42 countries since kindergarten.

"It's none of your business," I blurted back at him. "I think you are hurting, and you are trying to cover up."

"How many?" he threw it right back at me.

"What is the pain about?" I challenged back.

"How many?" he repeated.

I gave in. "One." I said. He didn't catch on I was talking about my wife.

He laughed. "One? One! I've gone all the way with 13. I think I know a little more about sex than you do."

"Maybe you do. What did you learn?" I asked.

"You wouldn't understand," he answered, dismissing me. His response led me to believe that he thought I was being sarcastic. I wasn't.

"What did you learn?" I repeated.

"Just forget it," he retorted.

"Fine," I replied. "I want to challenge you with the words you just used. I don't believe you went all the way." This ignited an explosion.

"The hell I didn't!" he shouted. "I had sex with these..."

I cut him off before he could finish "I know you had sex; I called those girls. But you didn't go all the way, because you don't even know what that is. Going all the way is emotional, psychological, spiritual, and intellectual.

"Going all the way is getting up at two in the morning with a crying baby when it is your turn. Going all the way is when you both hurt each other and instead of kissing good night, one of you says I did not like the way I was treated tonight and you both decide to talk this out. That is going all the way. What you have been doing is masturbating. You have been making love to yourself.

"What kind of relationships have you got? You can't even call these girls to tell them they are sick. My wish for you is that you slow down and quit playing all your games and really meet someone. Slow down and take the time to meet someone really, then go all the way emotionally, psychologically, spiritually, intellectually. I think you might find this more fulfilling."

I'd love to say this guy now is married, has eight kids, and is a deacon in the church. I honestly never saw him again. I have no idea what he is doing. I do believe, however, that God is not a killjoy. God graces us with the wonderful gift of sexuality. I believe God wants us to use this gift to go all the way in the real sense of this phrase.

I recall a conversation with my grandmother not long before she died. A friend had sent her a tape of a talk I gave on sexuality. She enjoyed the tape and went on to tell me that when she thought Grandpa was interested in sex, she would turn the crucifix and holy pictures the other way so that God would not witness this. I wanted to take her hand and say God was probably present in the room telling them, "Go for it. This is why I created it. This is going all the way."

This example also touches on the subject of the sacredness and beauty of sexuality. People in our culture use the phrase casual sex to describe using relationships. To people who sincerely value their sexuality, the phrase is a contradiction in terms. Casual sex implies that people engage in sexual activity (which could be anything from kissing to sexual intercourse) that means little or nothing to them. The phrase further implies that the persons having casual sex mean little or nothing to each other. This sex lacks love, energy, passion, and commitment. Casual sex seems like paying for front row seats at the concert of a favorite musical performer but only hearing the warm-up band.

There is nothing casual about how a human being gives herself or himself physically and mentally to another. Today when people seem caught up with how many partners they have had and how much sex, they are missing the point.

The number of times one has sex or the number of partners is no measure of intimacy. The quality and integrity of our relationships is the real measure. I believe most of us prefer to have a few meaningful, authentic relationships than rack up thousands that are empty and shallow in some sort of artificial contest. When we develop a deep intimacy and decide to marry, the sex will take care of itself. The reverse is not true. Sex will not teach us one thing about intimacy.

How do our desires for acceptance and love develop into unhealthy, destructive patterns? Pattern is the key word. A pattern is a repeated, habitual action, usually one so much a part of us that we can't see it.

Many young people who make a mistake sexually reflect on what happened, learn from it, and move on to healthier patterns. Their experience of being used or using someone—emotionally, mentally, or physically—helps motivate them to change their destructive patterns.

The young people who make a mistake but get quality help and support from family, friends, a minister, teacher, or counselor generally don't suffer any long-term consequences. They normally can learn from the experience and alter their negative patterns.

Jesus himself was quick to forgive the woman caught in adultery and called her to change her patterns in telling her to sin no more (John 8.1-8). God forgave King David when David recognized the wrong he had done in taking another man's wife (2 Samuel 12.1-25). People who make mistakes and work them through can avoid destructive patterns.

Patterns grow increasingly destructive in young people who don't see them but get used or use others again and again. These people

establish unhealthy patterns that injure present relationships and that they will carry with them into marriages and adult relationships. Their chances to experience healthy, authentic, intimacy are almost nil.

Authentic intimacy is so powerful an experience that every person deserves a chance at it. Everyone deserves to experience the powerful, passionate, redemptive energy of healthy sexuality and intimacy.

It is sad to hear 18- and 19-year-old men and women tell me that they never want to have sex again or get involved with someone because it is just a ripoff. Their feelings are a result of never having experienced true intimacy. They have been playing at it. They have never gone all the way. They have only gone through the motions.

At this point some readers may be feeling that this talk about feeling people up and having sex is way ahead of where they are at. "Buddy, I haven't even been on a date. Come back in five years and we will talk."

This is a legitimate reaction. However, what a person knows about intimacy has nothing to do with the number of dates or the amount of experience he or she has had. Some may have been on two dates but developed several intimate friendships. Others may have been on 600 dates and know nothing about intimacy, nothing about sharing who they are with another.

- After reading and discussing this chapter, reevaluate the three things you definitely do not want in your relationships.

- What genital, unhealthy patterns do you see in couples your age and also in adults?

- How can you or do you challenge people you care about when they get into unhealthy relationships?

CHAPTER 12

Integrated Intimacy

Integrated patterns of intimacy involve loving someone for who they are, not for what they do. Answer the following questions to begin reflecting on your own patterns of intimacy.

"Real love exists when your strong, tender feelings for the other are balanced by reason and deep respect. You care just as much for the other person's welfare and fulfillment as you do for your own. Judgments about the person are quite objective and rational."

—*Ray Short,* Sex, Love, or Infatuation*

---

*Ray E. Short, *Sex, Love, or Infatuation: How Can I Really Know?* Minneapolis: Augsburg Press, 1990.

WOMEN

1. *Do you have male and female friends that you can talk to?*
   Do you have male or female friends you can safely confide in?

2. *Do you have friends you trust enough to tell them something such as, "My parents seem to be fighting more. I am worried they may get a divorce." Does this person hold your hand and listen?*

3. *Do you have male and female friends with whom you can laugh and cry?*

4. *Do you have male and female friends who will touch you, hold you, or give you a hug when you need it?*

5. *Do you have friends who will give you grief in a fun way? Friends who tease you and you them?*

6. *Do you have female and male friends with whom you can be yourself? Do you have male and female friends whom you can go to McDonald's with and have so much fun they kick you out, and you didn't even do anything wrong? These are all signs of healthy, integrated patterns.*

MEN

1. *Do you have women and men friends you can talk to? Someone who would listen and care that the woman you have been dating for a year dumped you?*

2. *Do you have male and female friends whom you can hold and hug?*

3. *Do you have female and male friends to whom you can give grief, whom you can tease, and with whom you can flirt, and these people don't even want anything from you?*

4. *Do you have male and female friends with whom you can go dancing, go out for pizza, and just be yourself? Do you have female and male friends with whom you have such a good time that people stare at you?*

5. *Do you have friends with whom you can be yourself, laugh, and cry?*

If you answer yes to most of these or even some of these questions, then you know what integrated patterns of intimacy are. Integrated patterns of intimacy have much in common with being a good friend. The people we date, share ourselves with, and marry should also be good friends.

Sometimes teens will ask if I think they are into healthy or unhealthy patterns of intimacy. It is difficult to offer any meaningful insights to this question without knowing more about their personal situations, but four questions are always worth thinking about.

First, is the relationship fun? Second, is the relationship exclusive? Third, are we comfortable with silence? Fourth, am I dating an equal?

1. Dating is supposed to be fun.

I don't mean that every moment is hilarious. Sometimes couples need to do some serious talking, but generally dating should be fun. It should not be pressure. Relationships have no set patterns and timetables. In a healthy relationship, there is no point A, B, C, or K to get to. Two people enjoy being with each other. If one person in the relationship is not comfortable doing something, the other respects that. In a healthy relationship, one or both of the

people involved can say no and the other person will respect that, simply because the relationship is too important to risk hurting. In a healthy relationship people enjoy being with each other and don't pressure each other.

Most of us have observed couples who fight constantly. He puts her down behind her back, she puts him down behind his back, and friends wonder why they continue to go out.

100

The fun in the relationship has passed. Their relationship exists like a bad habit, or they are hanging on to each other until someone else comes along.

When couples constantly bad mouth each other or seem to genuinely dislike each other, it is time to take a break or end the relationship. The fun, the spark, the basic respect is gone. Sometimes couples go through a rough period and maintain respect for each other.

2. Relationships should not be exclusive.

Fun is a basic indicator of healthy patterns of intimacy; exclusivity signals an unhealthy pattern. Relationships that are healthy tend to include others and tend to be open to life. She is open to meeting his friends and trying new activities that he enjoys. He is open to meeting her friends and learning more about her interests.

When I observe couples cutting off family and friends, when they stop doing things they used to love doing, I get nervous that the relationship is becoming unhealthy. It can appear very romantic when he announces he is not trying out for the basketball team senior year, so he can spend more time with her. Often this is more foolish than romantic. If we sincerely love someone, we want them to be happy. We do not want to take from them the very things they enjoy doing. All relationships need time for people to be alone, but when this becomes the norm, it can be a danger sign. Healthy relationships tend to be inviting to others and energizing, not exclusive. In my experience, exclusivity is an indicator that sex is becoming a preoccupation in the relationship.

This can become a trap for the couple. When sex becomes the focus of the relationship, it isolates the couple from the very people and things they enjoy.

Watching males or females exclude their same-sex friends to the point of losing them is hard. Many times I have listened to teens mourn the loss of good friends whom they cut off while they were dating. Sometimes their dating relationship ends, and they have permanently lost touch with good friends. A person who really loves me does not ask me to give up friends I really care about. No one person, no matter how great she or he is, can take care of all my needs. To believe someone can fulfill all my needs is a naive, pseudo-romantic thought, not reality.

I have worked with adults, some married, whose relationships suffer from the exclusivity trap. Their relationship becomes suffocating for one or the other. In healthy relationships people want others to meet the person they love. They want the person they love to meet the other people in their lives, to interact, not to become isolated. Authentic love, includes, invites, is open to life and people. It does not desire to exclude or cut off the other people with whom they share life.

Once I was presenting a workshop on sexuality to a group of high school students. They were from large Midwestern cities: Chicago, Milwaukee, Gary, Indianapolis. I was discussing the concept of integrated patterns of sexuality, when a junior from Chicago asked if he could comment on something I presented.

"I don't go on dates anymore without having our talk first," he said. "I tell the girl what my limits are physically and why. I lay out my boundaries. If she can't respect those, then the date is over. If we start pushing beyond the boundaries, we call a timeout and have a good talk. The reason is that I loved this one girl more than any other. I got her pregnant, and her parents never let me see her again. It still hurts, and I will not let that happen again."

I was amazed. I affirmed him for this and said that I had never heard of teens setting boundaries like that. Out of the 100 kids in the workshop at least 20 more openly talked about setting boundaries. This is a sign of healthy intimacy.

3. **A third indicator, not proof, of healthy intimacy is that the couple is comfortable with silence.**

Silence can be a sign that the couple can't talk and the relationship is in jeopardy, but usually being silent together comes from a high level of comfort and trust.

Remember some of those wonderful first dates.

He picks her up to take her to the movie. She gets into the car.

"Hi. You look great," he says.

She thanks him. "You look good yourself."

Then silence. The silence of 30 seconds that can feel like an hour. He makes a left-hand turn.

CAN WE TALK
TOGETHER? CAN
WE BE SILENT
TOGETHER?

"That was a great left-hand turn," she blurts out. "Who did you take Driver's Ed. from? Oh, really? So did I."

Let's talk about something, anything!

Couples who are intimate in healthy ways can sometimes silently study together or sit closely together for 15 minutes or more and feel very comfortable. Fun, openness to others, and comfort with silence all indicate health in close, developing friendships. Basically, healthy patterns of intimacy show in the ability to be a friend. Anyone who has healthy friendships knows something about real intimacy. The people we date and eventually marry should be our good friends.

Those young people who have several healthy, intimate friendships but never seem to date should hang in there. Sometimes we feel as if all the jerks get dates. I had my annual date in high school. I was probably the Confirmation service project for some of them. It can feel as if everyone in America is dating but me. At times this can be funny; it can also be painful.

However, compromising one's self to get dates is not worth it. Some women hide their intelligence, their assertiveness, their humor so that they won't intimidate the guy. Some men will act like someone else, trying to be tough, funny, or intelligent, thinking the women will like them more. This is a natural tendency, but crazy. No date is worth the price of not being one's self. Good friendships with males or females are more life-giving than these kinds of dates.

In my years as a youth minister and campus minister, I have observed that some teens do not date much simply because they are mature enough to be themselves. They have enough inner strength not to play some of the games others play.

One high school senior came in to talk, feeling depressed because she had no dates. It was painful to listen to her wondering what was wrong with her and second guessing her personal worth because she had so much going for her. I could honestly look at her and say she definitely scared some guys off because she was her own person. She was honest, fun, and deep.

These very traits probably kept some guys away short term, but long term these traits will serve her well. I hoped she could understand that though she had fewer dates, at least those she had would be real. She could act phony, play games, and probably secure a few more dates, but were they worth the price? She answered no. But she needed support and reminding that the male and female friendships she had were of very high quality. She had great friendships.

We discussed women in her class who dated frequently because of their looks but who passionately desired the kind of friendships with men, as well as women, that she had. I believe that some of the people she was envious of were also jealous of her.

- How many of you have (or know of people who have) deliberately held back something about yourselves because you were afraid it might intimidate a person you were dating?

- Does this happen seldom, never, often? How can holding back eventually cause problems?

4. **Dating equals is a fourth indicator of healthy, integrated intimacy.**

Once in Colorado while giving a talk on intimacy to a group of Air Force chaplains, one of them asked, "I have a 22-year-old friend who recently found Jesus. He constantly has his Bible with him, wears huge crucifixes, and will preach to anyone who will listen and some who won't. He started dating a 17-year-old high school student. They got pregnant. He felt terrible. It was against everything he believed. She wanted to get married, but he feared it was just because of the pregnancy, and he convinced her not to. He also talked her out of an abortion, supported her through the entire pregnancy, the delivery, and the adoption. My question is, why after going through all of this, would he now start dating a 16-year-old?"

I do not know this person's friend. I only know what he told me. I did suggest that he ask the man if he was afraid of intimacy. By dating women younger than himself, he has control over how close they can get to him. Most younger women at this age cannot challenge him on the same intellectual or emotional level that women closer to his own age can. Consequently, he is safe. He doesn't have to let anyone in. He can avoid real intimacy. I wonder if he fears a woman who can stand toe to toe with him, who is capable of challenging him emotionally, psychologically, spiritually, and mentally.

Choosing to date someone who will be dependent and safe happens with more frequency than we think. I hear teens talk about women and men they go out with who are "so stupid" or "will never get it." Some guys will brag about the "bimbos" they date, and some girls about the "clueless" guys they go out with.

When I hear these remarks, I tend to think less of them than the people they are ridiculing. I want to challenge them, and sometimes do, by questioning them about what they are avoiding. I want them to reflect on why they consistently choose to date people they can control. Are they afraid someone might get in? Are they fearful of the vulnerability that real intimacy requires?

A woman whom I counseled went through a painful divorce. Her husband certainly played a role in the breakup. He steadfastly refused to go to counseling with her and to work on the marriage. I acknowledged that he appeared stuck and had his own stuff to work through. But what was her part? I pushed her to reflect on what she had to learn about herself from this experience.

She took this seriously, and after a number of sessions, she was able to share that she married him because he was safe. She knew he would never be able to get into her soul and who she was. He could never really hurt her. She opted for safety over vulnerability. When she desired the kind of intimacy she had avoided, he was incapable of responding or unwilling to give it. Real intimacy is not easy. It requires ongoing energy and effort. Avoiding intimacy is an easy pattern to develop early in life and one we can transfer into our adult relationships.

- Identify healthy relationships you see around you.
  What is healthy about them?
  Three things I definitely want in my relationships are....
  Something I struggle with in relationships is....

- Identify an older couple (21+) that you think have a good relationship. Ask them what keeps their relationship working. Report back to class.

- Invite a couple or two and some single people to form a panel to talk with your group about their marriages and relationships.

Aphrodisiacs, Drugs, and Sex

What is an aphrodisiac?
Have you heard of any,
such as green M&Ms?

"I had sex with somebody. I don't

remember who it was."

—*Anonymous Teen.*

Our society places more emphasis on sex than it does on intimacy.
Aphrodisiacs and drugs offer no shortcut to real, intimate relationships.

Many magazines offer to improve our sex lives or our love lives.
"Ten ways to be a better lover." "Eleven steps to better sex."
"Twelve easy steps to creating more exciting relationships."

Any time we are waiting in line at the grocery store checkout aisle, we can
take time to peruse the magazines on the rack. At least one of them will feature
new ways to enhance our sex lives. The sad reality is that people will spend $3 or
$4 for these.

People also put their faith and money into aphrodisiacs that promise better sex lives. A tragic example of this is the belief some men hold that the horn of the rhinoceros has the power to increase their virility, thus improving their sex lives. We continue to drive the rhinoceros to extinction so that these men can grind these horns into powder, which they digest to increase sexual prowess.

Let us leave reality for a brief moment and create a fictional woman or man whose goal in life is to be the sexiest human in the world. This person spends most of her or his life trying to have the perfect body, the perfect hair, the perfect smell, to be the best kisser in the history of the world. Perhaps this person even achieves some success. But if this perfect person forgets a friend's birthday, that may say more about his or her sexuality and capacity for intimacy than how he or she looks or kisses. If this great-looking person only talks about himself or herself and never asks about you, the relationship is one-sided and gets old really fast.

Learning about intimacy will serve us better in our relationships than articles on love lives, potions, or sexiness. Using drugs can be much more than a waste of money; using can endanger our lives.

MYTH

DRUGS OR
ALCOHOL
ENHANCE
SEXUALITY.

My counseling work is primarily in the areas of chemical dependency and sexuality. Unfortunately, I could probably make a living just working with victims of sexual abuse resulting from drug use. When I hear about a student or spouse who was physically or sexually abused and the circumstances in which the abuse took place, I automatically ask if the perpetrator was using any kind of drug at the time. The overwhelming response is yes. There are exceptions, but not many.

Time and time again, when a student or spouse is in danger of abuse, after following all the required procedures, I tell the person to get out of the house when the perpetrator is using. Take a walk, go to the park, a relative's, neighbor's, somewhere. Also take with you anybody else in the house who is in danger.

Studies report that anywhere from 23% to 47% of young people's first sexual experiences are alcohol or drug related. The wide disparity is the result of different studies. However, either one fourth or almost half is significant. There is little intimacy involved in sex associated with drug use.

"Yeah, I got laid last night at the party. I'm not sure who it was. I can't remember. I'm pretty sure it was a person."

This is pathetic, but all too common. Alcohol and drugs prevent users from being genuinely intimate with someone. Drugs and alcohol can hide feelings, mask vulnerability, and keep users distant from genuine intimacy.

I have never had or ever will have the power to stop teens from going to parties and using. Many teens will experiment with drugs despite warnings. However, I will submit a plea with young people not to be foolish. This is the public service announcement section of this book.

Anyone who is going to parties where alcohol and drugs are available and who is planning to partake should go with friends who care. Friends have to keep an eye on one another, especially on someone who gets high. Underage drinking is both illegal and dangerous. Too many parties include people whose main purpose in attending is to wait for others to get drunk or high so that they can take advantage of them. Those of us working with young people deal with party rapes far too frequently.

I was at a university in California doing a workshop on intimacy. I brought up the connection between drug use and sex. At the conclusion of the workshop, a woman asked to talk with me. She encouraged me to keep speaking about the drug and sex issue. She also invited me to tell her story whenever I spoke.

She was a beautiful woman, Hispanic, with long, dark hair and attractive, dark eyes. She had been elected homecoming queen of her high school. She never drank or had sex in high school. She claimed she was not a prude. She had a great time at parties without using, and she never met a guy she felt she was in love with.

She went on to college where she and some friends were invited to a fraternity party. Some guys discovered she had never been drunk and thought it would be fun to see what she was like when she was hammered. They began tempting her with beer, wine coolers, and drinks. She refused all their advances. One man said he respected her for not drinking and apologized to her for all the harassing she endured about it. He volunteered to get her anything she wanted as a peace offering. She requested a Diet Coke.

It will forever remain a mystery if what happened next was premeditated or not. Somewhere between getting the Coke and giving it to her, someone poured about a third of the soda out and replaced it with Everclear. Everclear is tasteless and odorless. She didn't catch on. Since she had never been drunk before and the first thing she drank was Everclear, the liquor hit her hard. Everclear is 90-100% alcohol. She got dizzy and then sick. She threw up in the bathroom, came back into the party, sat down on a chair, and slept.

The guy who gave her the drink felt bad and was afraid she might get sick again on the chair, so he moved her into the bedroom. He noticed how pretty she was and knew she was passed out, so he raped her while she was passed out on the bed. He returned to the party, got drunk, and started bragging to his friends about having sex with this great-looking woman. Eventually, six other guys went into the bedroom and raped her.

Her roommate began searching for her when she did not see her out at the party and discovered her in the bedroom. She noticed she had sperm and blood on her leg (the blood probably as result of a ripped hymen) and took her to the college clinic.

I could tell many similar stories. I plead with anyone who uses at a party to have someone looking out for her or him. Infinitely better, do not put yourself in this position. A former student of mine told me that his fraternity has taken this issue on. When they attend parties, they watch for men preying on drunk women and intervene. It goes on far too much.

WHEN SOMEONE IS HIGH, NOTHING MEANINGFUL CAN HAPPEN.

Drugs and alcohol can simply be another way of avoiding intimacy. When someone is high, she or he does not have the capacity to be authentically intimate. When someone is high, nothing meaningful can happen; there is no real rubbing of souls. The person can claim he or she wasn't in control. "I didn't know what I was doing."

Alcohol and drugs do not give anyone permission or an excuse to do anything. It is rape if someone has sex with someone who has passed out. It is rape if someone purposely gets another person drunk to take advantage of her or him. It is rape even if someone gets so drunk she or he consents to sex, knowing full well she or he would not have consented sober. Sure, nothing may happen legally. Proving rape in court may be a long shot, but what is legal is not always moral. Morally, raping someone is always wrong. Raping someone who is drunk is taking advantage of someone who has neither power to consent nor power to resist.

- What connection do you see between drugs and sex among your peers or the kids you hang around with?

- Do you think the number of first sexual experiences being alcohol or drug-related is closer to 25% or 50%?

- How many in the group have heard stories similar to the one above? How many women or men in the group have been hit on by someone who is drunk or high?

- How can drug or alcohol use get in the way of authentic intimacy?

CHAPTER 14

But If We Really Love Each Other...

Keep a record for a week of what attitudes toward premarital sex you see and hear—in songs, in ads, in films and videos, in conversations.

"Love will get you through times of no sex better than sex will get you through times of no love."
—Michael Johnson,
"Love and Sex"

The question of premarital sex comes up every year in the classes I teach and the workshops I conduct. The Catholic Church is very clear. Premarital sex is wrong. The Church reserves sex exclusively for marriage.

The Church has good reasons for its teaching. A man and woman who are dating have made no public commitment to mutual love and faithfulness. They are free to have sex today and break up tomorrow. They have no permanent relationship into which to welcome children and no family structure in which to raise them. The Church values the love that sex celebrates and considers sex between two people who love each other as sacred when exercised in marriage. Sex helps express love and faithfulness that a man and woman promise each other in marriage.

Most high school people I work with know what the Church teaches. They want to know why. Some accuse the Church of being "hung up on sex." Some are looking for a loophole to justify having sex. For most, just saying no is not enough help for the complex feelings, friendships, disappointments, and desires they are experiencing and sorting out.

Teens are struggling to integrate their sexuality and spirituality in the midst of conflicting cultural values. Many films, songs, and ads make sex seem the thing everyone is doing. Family and church say no. Teens have to grapple with these contradictions and their own new awareness of sexuality.

Young people often ask my personal opinion about premarital sex. I tell them they are asking the wrong question. I push and stretch the question toward the deeper issue—what makes an action right or wrong? What makes an act a sin?

I like to tell my students that kissing can be a sin. They are quick to attack this.

"Show us in the Bible where it says kissing is wrong."

"Show me in the Bible where it says cannibalism is wrong," I counter. The Bible does not have written rules for every choice we face today. However, Jesus makes clear in his Sermon on the Mount that he comes not to "abolish the law, but to fulfill it." He teaches not only the respect for others' lives, reputations, and property that the Ten Commandments teach, he calls us to love as he loves, to love even our enemies. Jesus moves the law from concern with externals to concern with the human heart and what motivates our choices.

Jesus is not into law for the sake of the law but for the reasons behind the law, its spirit. The scribes and Pharisees of Jesus' time accuse him of breaking the law when he heals people on the Sabbath. They regard healing as work. The third of the Ten Commandments teaches people to rest from work on the Sabbath and keep the day holy. Jesus insists God did not make people to keep the Sabbath but made the Sabbath for people, to revive and renew them as his

healing does. The scribes and Pharisees also confront Jesus for picking grain on the Sabbath when he and his disciples are hungry. "See here! Your disciples are doing what is not permitted on the Sabbath," they say. Jesus reminds them how King David's men, when they were hungry, entered the house of God and ate bread offered to God, bread only priests could eat. "Have you not read in the law how the priests on temple duty can break the Sabbath rest without incurring guilt? I tell you something greater than the temple is here. If you understood the meaning of the text, 'It is mercy I desire and not sacrifice,' you would not have condemned these innocent men. The Son of Man is indeed Lord of the Sabbath" (Matthew 12.1-8).

Perhaps an example can help clarify what Jesus is trying to teach. Suppose as you wait for a red light to change, you spot a young child about to crawl into the street from behind a parked car. You notice a car coming toward the child and determine the driver cannot see the child. Your instinct is to help. No cars are coming, but the light is red. You wait because it's the law. The car strikes the child before you get there.

This is making an idol of the law. If you can save the child by safely going through the red light, you should do it.

Jesus challenges the Pharisees to look both behind the law at its spirit and within themselves at their intentions. Jesus' Sermon on the Mount stretches the crowd, calling them to do more than play it safe and obey the Commandments. He invites them to live the spirit of the law—to love God, their neighbors as themselves, and even their enemies.

What does all this have to do with kissing? Everything. Kissing in some cultures is a greeting. Kissing can indicate a deep friendship. Kissing can be a sign of love and affection. It can indicate that a relationship is moving beyond a friendship. Kissing between a man and a woman may be a sign that the relationship is growing from a friendship to a dating relationship.

However, kissing can also be used to manipulate. One can use kissing to convince another person that one really cares about her or him, even if one doesn't. Let me give a personal and painful example that taught me how wrong it is to use another person.

Five of my friends and I spent most of one summer together. Three of us were male and three female. As the summer progressed, four of the friends became an item, leaving Maria and me as the only ones who were just friends. Good friends. All six of us often piled into one car and went to drive-in movies. Maria and I actually enjoyed the films until the others began making out. We felt very uncomfortable, went to the concession stand, talked, and took our time returning.

One night the couples began embracing and Maria lost it. She attempted to push them out of the car, still wrapped in each others' arms. Together, we lifted them out of the car onto the grass, between the microphones. I informed them that I would return for them within two working days.

I drove Maria home, and we ended up parked in her driveway, talking. When she said she needed to go in, she asked me to kiss her. This confused me. Before I could say anything, she said, "Can't you kiss a friend?"

This made sense. What was my hangup anyway? There is nothing wrong with kissing a friend. I moved to kiss her on the cheek but she turned her lips to receive the kiss. As I kissed her, she began to kiss me more passionately. Now I was in a dilemma.

If I pulled away in surprise, I would look like the prude of the year. If I went along, I was definitely saying we had more than a friendship. I took the coward's way out. I went along, but I can say in all honesty it was not at all exciting for me. I felt so stupid. We kissed until she broke it off.

"Good night. That was nice," she said as she got out of the car.

"It was," I lied. On the way to retrieve the other couples, I decided that what had just happened was just a freak occurrence. She simply had a hormone surge or something, and it was over.

Wrong. The next two times Maria and I were together, she initiated passionate kissing. The fourth time, I hesitated and she noticed.

"What's the matter?" she asked me.

"Nothing," I said too quickly, trying hard not to look flushed.

"You don't want to do this?" she asked.

I couldn't respond. My mouth opened, but nothing that made sense was coming out. She read my face.

"Oh, my God! You don't feel this way, do you? I am so embarrassed."

I quickly began concocting a lie to tell her that I did feel the same way, but she beat me to it.

"You don't feel the same way about me, do you?" she repeated. "So, what have you been doing, faking it?"

"No," I protested with no conviction.

Her entire face filled with anger.

"I don't believe this is happening. You have been faking it. You don't feel the same way, do you?" she demanded.

"I didn't want to hurt you...," I said. I wanted to make her feel better.

"Hurt me!" she screamed. "You think this doesn't hurt? I can't believe this."

I reached out my arm to hold her.

"Don't touch me!" she warned. "I feel so stupid," she said, climbing out of the car. She was now crying. She slammed the door and left.

I valued our friendship. I called Maria; I tried to see her, but for a week she refused to talk to me. Finally I was able to wear her down, and we had a long talk. I was able to save the friendship. I learned something about life in this. I learned how easy it is to lie with my body, how possible to lead someone on for one's own purposes. It is a pattern that can be improved and perfected. It was a pattern I didn't want. I almost lost a great friend because of it.

I believe that what I did was wrong. It was a sin. Sure, Maria had responsibility in what happened, too, but I want to focus on my part. I knew I was leading her on. I knew full well that she was thinking beyond a friendship, and I did not feel the same way. I played along and hurt her.

We are all capable of leading people on when it serves our purpose. I led Maria on so I wouldn't look stupid. We can also act as if the other person is very special, when all we want is for him or her to go further physically with us for our own gratification. To mislead someone deliberately for our own egos or pleasure is wrong. Even worse, it can become an ingrained pattern, a game we play so often and so well that it becomes a part of us. We don't even notice we are playing it any more.

This is dangerous. We need to have integrity at the heart of our relationships, not manipulation.

Once a high school girl came to me in tears. She had been going with a guy for a number of months and felt she was falling in love with him. He made sexual advances to her but stopped when she told him she was not comfortable with going that far. He stayed with her until the first time they had sex. Right after that, he had a friend deliver her a note. The note said that he did not want to see her anymore, that he never really liked her, and that she was not exciting sexually. It was over. He attended a different school than she, so avoiding her was easy.

His rejection stung her. She used me to yell at him. She was furious at him. "He used me." She was angry with herself for giving in to him. "How could I have been stupid enough to let him?" Looking back, she could see how he led her to believe she meant something to him when in reality all he wanted to do was get her in bed. Once he did, the conquest was over.

What added to her pain was that he did not even have the decency to tell her to her face. He gave someone a note. She heard from his friend that within days of dropping her, he had another girlfriend. It also hurt because she really cared about him. She genuinely loved him and felt like a complete fool. "I knew better than to let this happen," she lamented. "I always wanted the first time to be very special, and I just gave it away."

We talked about her pain, but also about her integrity. She had learned a painful lesson. She knew she should not have had sex with him; she experienced the deep hurt of being used. I tried to help her see that he was the real loser. She had given herself fully to someone, out of love. It was wrong, a painful mistake. At least her mistake, through shortsighted, was an honest one. His was not.

Her former friend manipulated her and lied to her. He lied with his body as well as his words. He led her to believe she was special and that everything they did together was meaningful to him. It was a lie.

The wrong or sin in this scenario is not only the sex but also the using of another human being. If every time he kissed her, talked to her, held her close, told her he cared, listened to her, his intentions were solely to get her to have sex with him, then each time he did this was sinful. He lied with his words, his body, his feelings.

In his parable of the prodigal son, Jesus shows a young man discovering the deep wrong at the heart of his actions. The young man demands his inheritance. His father gives it to him. The young man proceeds to waste the money on drinking, gambling, and loose women. How the son wastes his inheritance takes place in just one verse of the story. His sin is not only the drinking, gambling, and sex that take place in that verse but his turning his back on the father who loves him. He rejects all that his father believes. He rejects his father's love. He puts his attitude into action. He tells his father to get lost. I don't need you, care about you, or want you.

Human beings hav

What does this have to do with premarital sex? Again, everything. When someone asks me if premarital sex is wrong or right, I can say without hesitation the act is wrong, but judging the person is more difficult.

What about the case of a couple soon to be married? Their commitment is sincere, their love real. They engage in sex shortly before their marriage. Premarital sex is always wrong, but the degree of guilt may vary with circumstances. No one knows how deliberately the two decided to do wrong. Only God can judge their actions.

Human beings have the power to choose. A choice begins with an intention, a goal in mind, a good that will happen. An intention resides within the heart of each person. People's intentions must be taken into account when we are talking about sin. We can intend to love; we can intend to use.

To make moral choices, we need knowledge. We have an obligation to know what the Church teaches and why, to educate our consciences. We must dialogue with family, peers, and significant adults in our lives to gain from their experience. All of this contributes to seeking out God's will for us.

Some of my students are quick to say that if they determine sex is valid for them at this time in their lives, then they can have sex without sin. Wrong. It is not that easy.

Sin is still sin. Sex is a sacred act and cannot be treated lightly. Sex is easy to rationalize. It feels good. But having sex can hurt or destroy a relationship. If I really love someone, refraining from sex can be a greater act of love than having sex.

Students say they are mature and committed. They know their love is real. They will accept any consequences sex may bring, so sex is okay. Often the fact is their relationship cannot go any further without sex. My response is, "Don't have sex."

They protest. "You don't understand. We really love each other."

I challenge, "If you really love each other, then do not have sex. If your

relationship cannot go any further without sex, it is too dependent on sex."

A healthy, mature, relationship does not depend on sex; sex serves to celebrate the love in the relationship, but the love is not dependent on sex. Many married couples will experience times in this relationship in which sex is absent. The birth of a child can result in abstention from sex anywhere from weeks to months.

A couple who love each other may refrain from sex because they love each other. They realize sex can lead to a pregnancy; it can cause scandal to people they care about; it may lead to sex becoming a constant expectation or pressure that they don't want in their lives at this time. If a relationship cannot continue without sex, something is wrong. This point in a relationship is an excellent time to ask for help.

Intention, knowledge, and degree all come into play when we talk about what makes an action wrong. For an act to be a sin, a person must know the act is wrong and intend the consequences that result. A jury decides a person's guilt by taking the circumstances into account. The act of murder in itself is wrong. Few people in the world dispute this. However, does the person on trial know right from wrong? Was the murder premeditated? Was it in self-defense? Was it accidental? These are questions of knowledge and intent.

Degree is also important. If the guy who sent the it's-all-over note deliberately set the girl up in order to get sex from her, it was clearly wrong and sinful of him. Any intentional, deliberate use of another person for personal pleasure is wrong.

What gets more complicated are the "honest mistakes." There are teens I have worked with who sincerely believed they were in love at the time they engaged in sex. After thoughtful reflection, some of them realize they were not.

120

Love is not an exact science. They were rationalizing. Sometimes only pain makes consequences real.

After reflection, some realize they were not mentally together or healthy at the time, and they used other people sexually to try to make themselves feel better. Some realize that they simply wanted to experience sex, so they numbed themselves to their doubts, so they could keep doing what they were doing. For some of these teens and adults, sex is an addiction.

I am not condoning such sexual behavior. I do believe, however, that God will judge these people less harshly than the deliberate manipulators. Jesus himself was quick to forgive the woman caught in adultery. He challenged her to learn from getting caught and to sin no more. Teens who make mistakes sexually, especially honest mistakes, need to know that God forgives them.

Teens can learn from mistakes. It is important for teens to process what they experience with someone older whom they trust. This can be a source of healing. It also can be a way of intervening on unhealthy patterns that may prevent healthy relationships in the future.

Some teens, as well as some adults, rationalize that they are just having some fun until they have to settle down. Psychologists say that it can take two years to change a pattern. If we get into patterns of manipulating people, of lying to people we care about to get what we want, these patterns can become part of who we are.

It is very dangerous to think we have the ability to turn ourselves on and off when we please. Plus, what about the people we use? How many bodies will we leave wounded on our trails before we decide to get serious? We are establishing our patterns of intimacy right now. Are we establishing healthy or unhealthy patterns?

INTEGRITY IS AT THE HEART OF A GOOD RELATIONSHIP.

So, how can kissing be sinful? It is sinful if that kiss is not honest. If it means one thing to the receiver and another to the giver, the two need to talk. What is in the heart and mind of that kiss? Is the kiss honest or manipulative?

The same applies to sex. Is premarital sex always wrong? Yes, the Church says it is. But God and the Church also recognize the difference between honest mistakes and calculated choices. God and the Church recognize that there is a difference between a murderer who is sincerely sorry and a murderer who couldn't care less.

GOD ASKS THAT WE BE GOOD STEWARDS OF THE GIFT OF OUR SEXUALITY.

Most of the teens who talk to me about sexual issues do not come to ask if their sexual activity was right or wrong. Most of them already know something is wrong. They come to process what happened. They come to talk about what they learned or need to learn from what happened.

This is important. God knows all of us will make mistakes. What is important is to learn from them. Why did I get into this situation? Why did I let myself get used? What was I looking for in that relationship? Why am I lying to this person I claim to care about? Why did I want to believe the lies?

The more any of us can engage in self-reflection and can pray and process with healthy people, the better our chances are of not repeating our mistakes and of avoiding destructive patterns that can get in the way of healthy, authentic relationships.

God graces us with the gift of sexuality. As with all of creation, God asks that we be good stewards of what God has given us. We must learn to cherish, enjoy, and take care of this gift of sexuality.

- What is the difference between an honest mistake and a deliberate choice?

- What is an example of an honest mistake in your life? What did you learn from the experience?

- What convinces you premarital sex is wrong?

- What evidence can you gather that many people in our world view sex as sacred?

People Who Care

"As we are liberated from our own fear, our presence automatically liberates others."

—*Nelson Mandela, Inaugural Address*

What support do you need to wait until marriage to have sex?

Many teens express agreement with the principles and values in this book. However, some lament, "Everyone is doing it." They see little support for living up to their values. Sometimes this is an excuse, yet it is often real.

1. The first step in finding support is getting the facts straight.

Statistics about teens' sexual activity hit the headlines every so often. Editors make the headlines sensational to draw readers. So we read, "More teens than ever having sex."

Not everyone is having sex. Some statistics claim that over 50% of American youth have had sex by age 18. Other statistics place the figure at 40-45%. These percentages mean that half or more young people are not having sex. The headline could read, "Most teens not sexually active."

In recent research, the Search Institute placed the number of teens in Minnesota having sex by age 18 at 47%. A second statistic received surprisingly little publicity and deserved more—38% of the 47% had sex only once. This fact is important.

Most adolescents are not engaging in sex all the time. Yes, some are; but the vast majority are not. Not everyone is doing it. Those who are not having sex deserve affirmation and support from adults.

2. The second step for teens in finding support is making friends and finding mentors who share their values.

Friends influence and put pressure on each other. Friends who enjoy a variety of activities, have fun in groups, and work at sharing their real feelings help each other develop a capacity for intimacy and commitment. Friends who agree they will wait until marriage for sex support each others' commitments.

Adults are an important source of support for teens, too. Most young people appreciate adult mentors who are willing to talk with them and walk with them in their efforts to integrate their sexuality and their spirituality. They welcome parents, brothers, sisters, relatives, ministers, teachers, friends who ask them what is going on in their lives.

Of course, young people's real answers may not be what an adult wants to hear, nor will an adult's viewpoint be what a teen wants to hear. But real and honest communication is always difficult, never impossible, and very worthwhile.

TEENS WHO ARE NOT HAVING SEX DESERVE AFFIRMATION AND SUPPORT FROM ADULTS.

Teens have a right to expect adults to model real, healthy relationships. They watch how parents, teachers, and other adults interact—the language adults use when talking about sexuality, the ways men relate to women, and women to men. Teens test whether adults practice what they preach. Their questions challenge us adults to greater integrity in our own lives.

Finally, the Christian community holds ideals that support teens' growth toward intimacy. I respect the Church for holding up our sexuality as a gift from God that is good and holy. The Christian community calls all of us to wholeness and holiness. We have lifelong work in integrating body and spirit, assertiveness and vulnerability, words and mystery.

May we cherish our sexuality as God's gift, a sacred gift. May we denounce attempts to exploit, trash, or trivialize the gift. May we have the maturity to use our gift of sexuality to build and enhance our relationships and our world. May we go all the way in the full sense that God invites in marriage.

- Discuss with a partner what you would like to promise the person you marry.

SEXUAL MYTH TEST ANSWERS

1. False

2. False

3. True

4. True

5. True

6. False

7. False

8. False

9. False

10. True

11. False

12. True

13. False

14. False

15. False